Write the Greatest Essays

Essay Writing A to Z

STEP 1 **Essay Skills & Writing Skills**

Steve Brown · Hee Cho

saram**In**

What Is in This Book?

Whether you are writing an essay for a university assignment, for TOEFL or for IELTS, you are often answering the same type of question. You might need to give your opinion, agree or disagree with something, or compare some advantages and disadvantages. This book shows you the key skills you need to write each type of essay, how to structure your answers, and how to write clearly and efficiently.

Why Is This Book Different from Other 'Essay Writing' Books?

1

Each unit examines real essays and passages written by Korean students of English.

2

Each unit contains multiple exercises in addition to a step-by-step guide regarding the topic.

3

The book is equally useful as a textbook for teachers or as a self-study workbook.

Who Is This Book for?

This book is aimed at intermediate level students of English who:

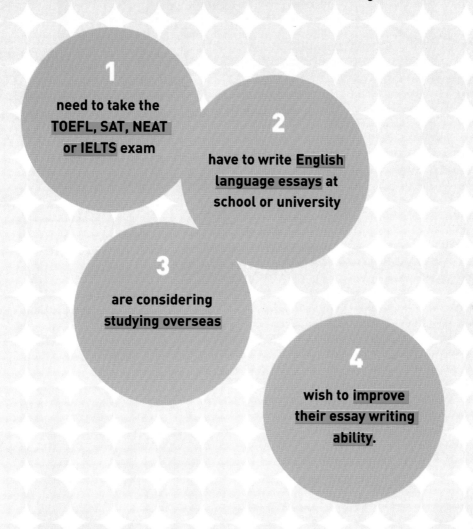

1 need to take the TOEFL, SAT, NEAT or IELTS exam

2 have to write English language essays at school or university

3 are considering studying overseas

4 wish to improve their essay writing ability.

The book assumes you can read, understand and write English at an intermediate level, and it assumes you already know terms such as 'brainstorming' and 'outlining.'

How Is the Book Structured?

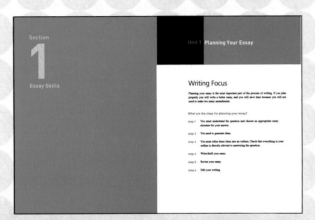

Section 1 Essay Skills looks at the basics of planning and structuring your essay. It focuses on how to write the different parts of an essay (introduction, body paragraphs, conclusion), and the key skills required for each.

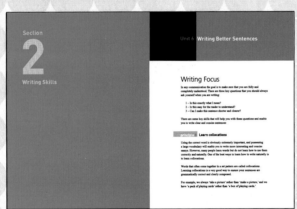

Section 2 Writing Skills looks at how to improve your essay writing. It looks at everything from common errors to writing academically.

How is Each Unit Structured?

Writing Focus
provides an **easy-to-understand explanation** of the topic.

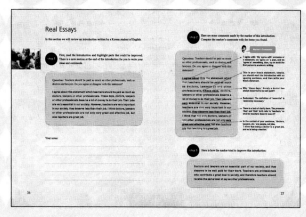

Real Essays
examines the writing of a Korean student of English.

Essential Skills
looks at **the essential skills needed for the topic.**

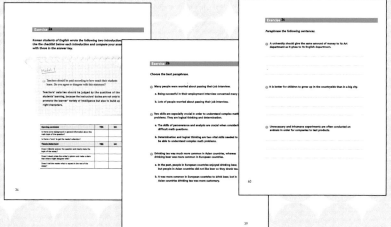

Multiple Exercises
helps you understand the topic and gives you **a chance to practice the topic.**

At the back of the book there is an Answer Guide **that provides not only the answers to the exercises, but also comprehensive explanations.**

Thank you!

This book contains sentences, passages and essays written by Korean learners of English. These students generously agreed to allow us to use their writing so that others may improve their English ability.

We would like to say a big 'thank you' to:

Seung Min	Hyo Jae	Sun Ho	Seu Reo Woon
Seung Eun	Jeong Jun	Da Eun	Ji Su
Hae Rim	Nan Hee	Jeong Whan	Min Hyeok
Da Hyeong	Yoo Kyung		

Steve Brown & Hee Cho

Section1 Essay Skills_13

Section 2 Writing Skills _99

Section 1 **Essay Types 1** _13

Section 2 Essay Types 2 _97

Essay Skills

Section

1

Essay Skills

Writing Focus

Planning your essay is the most important part of the process of writing. If you plan properly you will write a better essay, and you will save time because you will not need to make too many amendments.

What are the steps for planning your essay?

step 1   You must understand the question and choose an appropriate essay structure for your answer.

step 2   You need to generate ideas.

step 3   You must refine these ideas into an outline; Check that everything in your outline is directly relevant to answering the question.

step 4   Write/draft your essay.

step 5   Revise your essay.

step 6   Edit your writing.

It is absolutely vital that you fully understand what the question is actually asking. It does not matter how well you write English if you do not answer the question correctly and completely. Look at this question:

> Q: In many countries, obesity levels in children are increasing. Explain why this is happening and what the implications are. Suggest some possible solutions.

There has to be three parts to your answer:

❶ You must explain why obesity levels in children are increasing.
❷ You must explain the implications of this situation.
❸ You must suggest possible solutions.

By carefully looking at the question you will ensure you answer it properly, and you will also get clues for the structure of your essay. In this case a possible structure would be:

▶ **Introduction**
▶ **Body paragraph 1** – explanation
▶ **Body paragraph 2** – implications
▶ **Body paragraph 3** – solutions
▶ **Conclusion**

The exact content and structure of your essay will change depending on the type of question you are answering, but it will always follow the same basic framework:

▶ an introduction, body paragraphs, and a conclusion

Examine this sample introduction that was written by a Korean student of English. Then answer the following questions. Check your answers with the answer key at the back of the book.

Q: Language and culture are respected less in comparison with the past. Do you agree or disagree?

Importance of language and culture is a big issue these days in that world is getting smaller by corresponding each other closely more than before. Some people argue that this issue will be faded in the future because it comes from less contact of people who are living in another area before globalization. However, language and culture are important to understand each other. It is certain that having more information about characteristics of another language and culture make people easy to understand each other more. This essay will manage why language and culture should be respected, although world is getting smaller.

❶ **This introduction does not directly answer the question. Write the reason(s) why it does not answer the question:**

....

....

....

....

2 **Examine the question and choose which of the following essay structures would be the most appropriate:**

a.

```
                    Introduction
                        ⬇
        Body 1 – agree (or disagree) point 1
                        ⬇
        Body 2 – agree (or disagree) point 2
                        ⬇
                    Conclusion
```

b.

```
                    Introduction
                        ⬇
            Body 1 – reasons for agreeing
                        ⬇
          Body 2 – reasons for disagreeing
                        ⬇
                    Conclusion
```

The most common types of questions in TOEFL and IELTS can be categorized into six broad categories. By looking at the vocabulary used in the question you can get clues as to the type of essay required.

Type of Questions	Examples
Cause and Effect	What are the reasons and results of...? Why is this happening and what are the consequences? Discuss the causes and effects of... Discuss the causes for this phenomenon. What causes this and what are the implications? Explain why this is happening and what the implications are?
Advantages and Disadvantages	What are the advantages and disadvantages of...? Discuss both the advantages and disadvantages of...
Compare and Contrast	Compare these two... Compare this with/to... Compare X with/to Y Compare and contrast X with/to Y Contrast... What are the similarities and differences...?
Opinion	Why is/are...? How can/could...? How is/does...? Do you...? What is the most important...? Why do you think...? What can be...? Has this...? Suggest... Give specific reasons supporting this viewpoint. Defend this statement with at least two reasons. Why is this?
Preference	Which do you prefer? Which of these do you recommend? Which do you think is better? Which would you choose?
Agree or Disagree	Do you agree or disagree...?

We will look at how to answer these types of questions in STEP 2, Units 1 to 6.

Look at the following questions and decide which type of question it is. Some of these questions may contain more than one type.

agree/disagree	cause/effect	opinion
compare/contrast	preference	advantages/disadvantages

1. Nowadays, food has become easier to prepare. Has this change improved the way people live? Use specific reasons and examples to support your answer.

....

2. Despite improvements in vehicle technology, there are still large numbers of road accidents. Explain some of the causes of these accidents, and suggest some measures that could be taken to address the problem.

....

3. A company has announced that it wishes to build a large factory near your community. Discuss the advantages and disadvantages of this new influence on your community. Do you support or oppose the factory? Explain your position.

....

4 Water is a natural resource that should always be free and governments should ban the sale of bottled water. Do you agree or disagree?

....

5 Some people like to travel with a companion. Other people prefer to travel alone. Which would you choose? Use specific reasons and examples to support your choice.

....

6 Compare and contrast living alone to living with your family. Use specific reasons and details to develop your essay.

....

Generating ideas for your essay

Once you understand the question you need to think how you are going to answer the question and what details you will include.

Whatever technique you use to generate ideas (such as brainstorming, mind-mapping, or free writing) is your choice. However, there are some requirements common to all these techniques that you must follow:

- ▶ Write the question on the top of your piece of paper.
- ▶ Try to decide your position first. Do you agree or disagree? Which of the suggestions do you prefer, etc.
- ▶ Then note down any points that you think of. At this stage it does not matter if the points are relevant or not, or in what order you note them down.
- ▶ Then, review your ideas in relation to the question. Delete any ideas that are not directly relevant.

Exercise 1c

❶ Generate some ideas for the following question in less than 5 minutes:

Q: Language and culture are respected less in comparison with the past. Do you agree or disagree?

Agree or disagree:
Ideas:

❷ Now, look at your ideas and highlight only those that are <u>directly relevant</u> to the question.

step 3 Creating an outline

After you have understood the question, thought about a possible structure for your essay, and generated some ideas for your answer, you can create an outline.

You do not have to write complete or correct sentences at this stage – your goal is to make sure that you know exactly what you will write in each part of the essay.

Look at this example outline (We will look at thesis statements, topic sentences etc. in detail in the next few units – a thesis statement is a sentence that tells the reader what your essay is about and must answer the question; a topic sentence tells the reader what a paragraph is about).

> Q: Traffic congestion is becoming a huge problem for many major cities. Suggest some measures that could be taken to reduce traffic in big cities.

Introduction	Thesis statement:	Reduce traffic in cities by better public transport and higher cost of using one's own car.
Body paragraph 1	Topic sentence:	People would use their cars less if public transport were more convenient.
	Detail:	Buses too infrequent, trains break down often.
Body paragraph 2	Transition:	Furthermore,
	Topic sentence:	Raising cost of motoring would deter excessive car use.
	Detail:	People use cars for small journeys e.g. local store.
Conclusion	Summarize your opinion or suggest a solution	Improving public transport and making motoring more expensive could be effective in easing traffic congestion in cities.

Exercise 1d

Look at the following question and suggested outline. Highlight any parts of the outline that are not directly relevant to the question. See the answer key at the back of the book to check your answers.

Q: Online shopping is increasing dramatically. How could this trend affect our environment and the kinds of jobs required?

Introduction	Thesis statement:	Online shopping has many advantages—goods getting cheaper and cheaper; benefits the environment.
Body paragraph 1	Topic sentence:	Less overheads therefore goods are cheaper.
	Detail:	Because goods are cheaper people can have lower-paid jobs and still be able to buy things.
Body paragraph 2	Transition:	Secondly,
	Topic sentence:	Online shopping is good for the environment.
	Detail:	Less packaging and less shoppers travelling.
Conclusion	Summarize your opinion or suggest a solution	Online shopping is definitely increasing and is good.

Exercise 1e

Use the ideas you generated in Exercise 1c to create an essay outline. Make sure you check your outline to ensure everything is relevant to the question. See the answer key at the back of the book for a suggested outline.

> Q: Language and culture are respected less in comparison with the past. Do you agree or disagree?

Introduction	Thesis statement:	
Body paragraph 1	Topic sentence:	
	Detail:	
Body paragraph 2	Transition:	
	Topic sentence:	
	Detail:	
Conclusion	Summarize your opinion or suggest a solution	

step 4 Writing/drafting your essay

You should not start to write your essay until you are completely happy with your outline. How to write an essay is covered in this book:

- ▶ Units 2 to 5 look at how to write the different parts of an essay.
- ▶ Units 6 to 9 look at some ways to improve your writing.
- ▶ STEP 2, Units 1 to 6 look at how to answer the different types of essay questions.

step 5 Revising your essay

This is the process of checking that everything you have written is:

- ▶ relevant to the question
- ▶ ordered logically
- ▶ clear and concise

In this stage you will often move entire paragraphs, delete whole passages and completely rewrite sentences. Revising is one of the most important steps to writing a good essay.

After you have written your draft essay, unless you can tick 'yes' to all of these questions you probably need to revise your writing.

Revision checklist:

Item	YES or NO	If no, what action should be taken?
Does my thesis statement directly answer the question?		Rewrite the entire essay
Does everything in the essay support the thesis statement?		Delete irrelevant items
Have all the components of an essay been included, such as topic sentences, a conclusion, etc.?		Add missing items
Have you avoided repeating points and ideas?		Delete the duplication
Do all the points/ideas follow a logical order?		Rearrange the order

Use the checklist to evaluate this passage written by a Korean student of English. Check your answer with the answer key at the back of the book.

Item	YES	NO
Does the thesis statement directly answer the question?		
Does everything in the essay support the thesis statement?		
Have all the components of an essay been included, such as topic sentences, a conclusion, etc.?		
Has the writer avoided repeating a point more than once?		
Do all the points follow a logical order?		

Q: Smoking should be banned in public places. Do you agree or disagree?

In today's society, smoking people have lost their smoking area especially in public place. Some people argue that this action is necessary for remaining people. On the other hand, others assert that despoil the smoking area even in public places is the same as deprive the freedom of smokers. This essay will deal with why smokers do not have the right of saying freedom in public places.

Firstly, given smoke can has terrible impact on the others, it is certain that reduce the smoking areas especially in public places such as popular squares or bus stops. If there are smoking areas in public place, many people will be suffered from smoke consist of diverse harmful ingredients such as CO or Nicotine. Priority non-smokers' liberty should be the first instead of keeping the minority smokers' freedoms.

Finally, depriving the place to smoke in public place can help decreasing the number of potential smokers. It is true that children can be affected easily by their surroundings. Seeing the scheme of smoking in public place might be the same as encourage children to smoke in the future. Regulation smoking area in public will be the best obstacle of smoking to prevent people from getting harmful ingredients such as Nicotine.

In conclusion, smoking areas in public should disappear for smokers, non-smokers and also children.

Editing your writing

This is the step of proofreading for grammar, punctuation and spelling. It is the final step before you submit your essay.

Exercise 1g

A Korean student of English wrote the following passage. Edit this writing for grammar, spelling and punctuation. Check your answer with the answer key at the back of the book.

> Online shopping could contribute to protecting environment from pollution. In fact, all environmental components, such as fresh water, air and earth, are usually polluted by a large number of vehicles. Online shopping would discourage people from using those kinds of vehicles, because the Internet allows shoppers to search what they want at the home, they do not need to use vehicles for moving. For example, if people do not go to shopping outside, the amuont of using car, bus, or taxi would be decresed. The shoppers could help nature by using online shopping.

Your notes:

....

....

....

....

....

Writing Focus

The introduction is the most important part of your essay. A poorly written introduction will lose the reader's interest and damage the credibility of your essay.

What must an introduction do?

▶ It must provide some interesting background information about the topic of the essay.

▶ It must 'hook' the reader's attention.

▶ It must clearly state the topic of the essay.

▶ It must contain a strong thesis statement.

How do I structure an introduction?

▶ First, write an opening sentence. This should 'hook' the reader's attention and provide some general or background information about the topic of the essay.

▶ Second, write your thesis statement.

What is a hook?

▶ A 'hook' is a sentence in your introduction that interests and engages your reader. A good 'hook' will make sure your reader continues reading your essay.

A hook is often:

• A surprising fact that the reader is unlikely to know

• A question for the reader to consider

• A bold or controversial statement that might cause an emotional reaction

• A definition of a word or phrase

• A quotation or well-known phrase

What is a thesis statement?

▶The thesis statement states the purpose and reason you are writing your essay. It must clearly state the topic of your essay and your opinion on the topic. Make sure your thesis statement:

❶ Directly answers the question and clearly states the topic of the essay.
❷ Clearly states your opinion and makes a claim or provides details that the reader might either agree with or dispute.
❸ Tells the reader what to expect in the rest of your essay.

Examples of good and bad thesis statements:

Too vague

🙂 Most TV programmes are poor quality.

😊 Most of the programmes shown on TV nowadays contain too much violence and bad language.

A poor opinion or claim

🙂 Drugs are available to help fight many diseases.

😊 If people are denied drugs their illnesses may not be easily cured, so it is imperative that everybody should have access to every available medicine.

Does not tell the reader exactly what to expect in the essay

🙂 James Maxwell was a great scientist.

😊 James Maxwell was a magnificent scientist. Not only did he formulate electromagnetic theory, he was also the first person to take a color photograph.

Let's *analyze* an introduction

Q: Teachers should be paid according to how much their students learn. Do you agree or disagree with this statement?

[A]Are teachers paid enough? [B]It is critical for teachers to provide a great education to their students, and therefore is vital that teachers' remuneration reflects their importance in society.
[C]However, a teacher's remuneration should not be dependent on how much their students learn for the following two reasons.

A This is the 'hook.' It asks a question to get the reader to think about your topic.

B This is the opening sentence. It has a 'hook' to get the reader's attention, and provides background information and general discussion of the topic.

C This is the thesis statement. It directly answers the question, clearly gives the writer's opinion, and tells the reader what to expect in the essay i.e. two reasons supporting the writer's opinion.

Korean students of English wrote the following two introductions. Use the checklist below each introduction and compare your answers with those in the answer key.

Model 1

Q: Teachers should be paid according to how much their students learn. Do you agree or disagree with this statement?

Teachers' salaries should be judged by the qualities of the students' learning, because the instructors' duties are not only to promote the learner' variety of intelligence but also to build up right characters.

Opening sentence	YES	NO
Is there some background or general information about the main topic of the question?		
Is there a 'hook' to get the reader's attention?		
Thesis statement	**YES**	**NO**
Does it directly answer the question and clearly state the topic of the essay?		
Does it clearly state the writer's opinion and make a claim that others might disagree with?		
Does it tell the reader what to expect in the rest of the essay?		

Q: Teachers should be paid according to how much their students learn. Do you agree or disagree with this statement?

Teachers in class can be a model in students' life. Thus, teachers should not be evaluated by the payment only according to the quantity of students' learning for the following two reasons: teachers' role as an adviser and rapport amid teachers.

Opening sentence	YES	NO
Is there some background or general information about the main topic of the question?		
Is there a 'hook' to get the reader's attention?		
Thesis statement	YES	NO
Does it directly answer the question and clearly state the topic of the essay?		
Does it clearly state the writer's opinion and make a claim that others might disagree with?		
Does it tell the reader what to expect in the rest of the essay?		

Real Essays

In this section we will review an introduction written by a Korean student of English.

step 1 First, read the introduction and highlight parts that could be improved. There is a note section at the end of the introduction for you to write your ideas and comments.

Question: Teachers should be paid as much as other professionals, such as doctors and lawyers. Do you agree or disagree with this statement?

I agree about this statement which teachers should be paid as much as doctors, lawyers or other professionals. These days, doctors, lawyers or other professionals deserve a lot of money to do their job. Their jobs are very essential in our society. However, teachers are very important in our society, they deserve less than their job. I think doctors, lawyers or other professionals are not only very great and effective job, but also teachers are great job.

Your notes:

....

....

....

....

step 2 Here are some comments made by the marker of this introduction. Compare the marker's comments with the items you found.

 Marker's Comments

Question: Teachers should be paid as much as other professionals, such as doctors and lawyers. Do you agree or disagree with this statement?

~~I agree about~~ this the statement ~~which~~ that teachers should be paid as much as doctors, lawyers ~~or~~ and other professionals. These days, doctors, lawyers or other professionals deserve a lot of money to do their job. Their jobs are ~~very~~ essential in our society. However, teachers are ~~also~~ very important in our society, they deserve less than their job. I think that ~~not only~~ doctors, lawyers ~~or~~ and other professionals are ~~not only~~ very great and effective jobs, but also ~~teachers are~~ that teaching is a great job.

- 'I agree with.' We 'agree with' someone or a statement, we 'agree on' a plan, and we 'agree to' something. Also, try to avoid the first person in academic writing.

- This is your thesis statement. Ideally, you should start the introduction with an opening sentence, and then write your thesis statement.

- Why 'these days.' Surely a doctor has always deserved to be well paid?!

- Redundant. The definition of 'essential' is 'absolutely necessary.'

- There is a lack of clarity here. The pronouns 'they' and 'their' both refer to 'teachers,' so what do teachers deserve less of?

- In the context of your sentence, 'doctors, lawyers, etc.' are people, not jobs. 'I think that <u>being a</u> doctor is a great job, and so is <u>being a</u> teacher.'

step 3 Here is how the marker tried to improve this introduction:

Doctors and lawyers are an essential part of our society, and they deserve to be well paid for their work. Teachers are professionals who contribute a great deal to society, and therefore teachers should receive the same level of pay as other professionals.

Essential Skills

What is paraphrasing?
▶ When you paraphrase a text, you restate the source text in different words.

How do you paraphrase something?
▶ You must keep the same meaning as the source text, but you must not copy. You must rearrange the text, and use different words, to say the same thing as the source text.

Why do I sometimes need to paraphrase for my introduction?
▶ Your introduction must clearly state the topic of your essay and directly answer the question. Often, the easiest way to do this is to paraphrase the question.

Let's *analyze* a paraphrase

Teachers should be paid according to how much their students learn.

➡ The amount that a student learns should determine how much a teacher is paid.

In the paraphrase, the meaning of the first sentence has not changed, but the structure and vocabulary are different.

Exercise 2b

Choose the best paraphrase.

❶ Many people were worried about passing their job interview.

    a. Being successful in their employment interview concerned many people.

    b. Lots of people worried about passing their job interview.

❷ Two skills are especially crucial in order to understand complex math problems. They are logical thinking and determination.

    a. The skills of perseverance and analysis are crucial when considering difficult math questions.

    b. Determination and logical thinking are two vital skills needed to be able to understand complex math problems.

❸ Drinking tea was much more common in Asian countries, whereas drinking beer was more common in European countries.

    a. In the past, people in European countries enjoyed drinking beer, but people in Asian countries did not like beer so they drank tea.

    b. It was more common in European countries to drink beer, but in Asian countries drinking tea was more customary.

Paraphrase the following sentences.

❶ **A university should give the same amount of money to its Art department as it gives to its English department.**

....

....

....

❷ **It is better for children to grow up in the countryside than in a big city.**

....

....

....

❸ **Unnecessary and inhumane experiments are often conducted on animals in order for companies to test products.**

....

....

....

Skill B: Writing thesis statements

Remember, a thesis statement must state the topic of the essay, it must directly answer the question, it must give an opinion or details that the reader may dispute, and it must tell the reader what to expect in the rest of the essay.

Exercise 2d

Choose the best thesis statement.

1 a. There are some good and bad features about going on a diet to lose weight.

   b. It is more important to eat healthy and nutritious foods than to try to lose weight quickly by going on a diet. A weight-loss diet can be dangerous, and often people gain the weight back once they stop the diet.

2 a. A business could use the Internet to promote itself, and a well-designed web page can be a great advertisement for the following two reasons.

   b. A business needs to use the Internet. A well-designed web page is a great way for a business to promote itself for the following two reasons.

3 a. Global warming is caused by many factors and has numerous effects that are bad for the planet.

   b. Global warming exists because of the overuse of fossil fuels and the huge number of cars in the world. Global warming leads to extreme weather conditions and rising sea levels.

Write a thesis statement for each of these topics.

1 The 1920s saw major changes in the world of fashion. What were the main developments and how have they influenced the fashion of today?

....

....

....

2 Downsizing is beneficial to companies. Do you agree or disagree?

....

....

....

3 Nowadays, food has become easier to prepare. Has this change improved the way people live? Use specific reasons and examples to support your answer.

....

....

....

Further Practice

Write a complete introduction for each of these questions.
Make sure your thesis statement has at least two specific ideas/opinions.
Then use this checklist to evaluate each introduction.

Opening sentence	YES	NO
Is there some background or general information about the main topic of the question?		
Is there a 'hook' to get the reader's attention?		
Thesis statement	**YES**	**NO**
Does it directly answer the question and clearly state the topic of the essay?		
Does it clearly state the writer's opinion and make a claim that others might disagree with?		
Does it tell the reader what to expect in the rest of the essay?		

1 **There should be more boys-only and more girls-only schools. Do you agree or disagree?**

2 How do movies or television influence people's behavior? Use reasons and specific examples to support your answer.

3 Compare and contrast knowledge gained from experience with knowledge gained from books.

Writing Focus

After you have written your introduction you begin the main body of your essay. For most IELTS or TOEFL essays, you will write two body paragraphs.

What must a paragraph contain?

▶ Each paragraph must only contain one main idea.
▶ The content of each paragraph must be directly related to your thesis statement.
▶ There must be sufficient support for your argument or point.
▶ There must be a topic sentence and a concluding sentence.

How do I structure a paragraph?

▶ First, write a topic sentence.
▶ Second, expand your argument by providing more detail, information and examples that are relevant to your position.
▶ Third, write a concluding sentence.

What is a topic sentence?

▶ The topic sentence is often the first sentence of a paragraph and it tells the reader the subject of the paragraph. Make sure your topic sentence:

- summarizes what the paragraph is about.
- controls the paragraph. Everything that is written in your paragraph should relate directly to the topic sentence.
- does not contain too much detail; the details of your argument follow the topic sentence.
- is directly related to your thesis statement.

Let's *analyze* a topic sentence

A cosmetics company sells its products by appealing to a person's desire to look younger.

The topic sentence tells the reader exactly what the paragraph will be about, but in summary form. It 'controls' the paragraph as the reader will expect to read details about how cosmetic companies sell their products, specifically related to people's desire to look youthful.

Good and bad topic sentences:

There are two ideas in this topic sentence

😐 Every student should have ❶access to a computer, and ❷teachers should be trained in how to use technology in the classroom.

😊 As technology in the classroom becomes more commonplace, it is essential that teachers receive adequate training in its use.

Too much detail

😐 Reading a fiction book provides people with many benefits. By learning to use their imagination people can become more creative, which could even lead them to inventing some wonderful new gadgets in the future.

😊 Reading good fiction novels can enhance a person's creativity.

Exercise 3a

A Korean student of English wrote the following topic sentences. Use the checklist below each topic sentence and compare your answers with those in the answer key.

1

First, mobile phones' main purpose is to contact people who are far away, but now these days when you see young teenagers use the mobile phone, they usually use the phone for text messaging and talking with very small reasons such as just wanting to chat with that person.

Topic sentence	YES	NO
Is the topic sentence a summary of what the paragraph will be about?		
Does it control the paragraph?		
Has it excluded details?		

2

Another reason that using a mobile phone is not good is that it may be dangerous for health.

Topic sentence	YES	NO
Is the topic sentence a summary of what the paragraph will be about?		
Does it control the paragraph?		
Has it excluded details?		

What is a concluding sentence?

▶ The concluding sentence of each paragraph finalizes the information in the paragraph, but it must not repeat what has already been stated.

▶ The two most common types of concluding sentences are:

- a paraphrase of the topic sentence that also adds the main details from the information in the paragraph. Use this type of concluding sentence if you do not need to give an opinion or express a preference.
- one that gives a definitive position or explanation based on the information contained in the paragraph. Use this type of concluding sentence if you need to give an opinion or express a preference.

▶ Make sure your concluding sentence:

- does not contain any new information.
- does not just repeat what has already been written.
- is directly related to your topic sentence.

Let's *analyze* the two main types of concluding sentences

Type 1_ a paraphrase of your topic sentence + main details

Topic sentence: A cosmetics company sells its products by appealing to a person's desire to look younger.

Example concluding sentence:
A cosmetic company understands people's aspirations to stop the ageing process and uses pretty models to convince people to buy its creams and treatments.

This concluding sentence paraphrases the topic sentence and adds some detail (pretty models) that would have been mentioned in the paragraph. It does not give any opinion or preference.

Type 2_ a concluding sentence that gives a definitive position or explanation

Topic sentence: A cosmetics company sells its products by appealing to a person's desire to look younger.

This concluding sentence makes a concluding remark/ position. You would use this type of concluding sentence if you were asked to give your opinion on the way a cosmetic company sells its products.

Example concluding sentence:
The techniques often used by a cosmetic company to sell its creams and treatments amount to false advertising and are immoral.

Korean students of English wrote the following concluding sentences. Use the checklist below each example and compare your answers with those in the answer key at the back of the book.

Topic sentence:
Firstly, teachers, as competent advisors in class, help students to improve their level of study through collaborative learning.

Concluding sentence:
Hence, whenever students have some curiosity while they are studying, a teacher will be there as a resource person.

Concluding sentence	YES	NO
Is the concluding sentence directly related to the topic sentence?		
Does it rephrase the topic sentence without adding new information?		
Does it avoid simply re-writing what has already been stated?		

②

> Topic sentence:
> **First, the teacher gives feedback to the students when they learn English productive skills like speaking and writing.**
>
> Concluding sentence:
> **So, the learners can recognize the right usage of collocations.**

Concluding sentence	YES	NO
Is the concluding sentence directly related to the topic sentence?		
Does it rephrase the topic sentence without adding new information?		
Does it avoid simply re-writing what has already been stated?		

NOTE: In Unit 4 we will look at how to write the detail and support for each paragraph.

Real Essays

In this section we will review a paragraph written by a Korean student of English, focusing on the topic and concluding sentences.

step 1   First, read the paragraph and highlight parts that could be improved. There is a note section at the end of the paragraph for you to write your ideas and comments.

Question: Some people think they can learn better by themselves than with a teacher. Others think that it is always better to have a teacher. Which view do you prefer?

Secondly, teachers intrinsically motivate students to keep studying subjects. By themselves, they can lose interest in their studies, unless the subjects are directly related to their daily lives. However, in school, teachers will stimulate students' interest in class by giving today's aim of the class and various educational materials. For example, before a speaking activity, a teacher can play a recorded dialogue as a listening material in which native English speakers are having a conversation about some topic, and then s/he will say to the students, "later this class, you can communicate this topic in 'native-like intonation' just like the people in the tape."

Your notes:

....

....

....

step 2 Here are some comments made by the marker of this paragraph. Compare the marker's comments with the items you found.

Marker's Comments

Question: Some people think they can learn better by themselves than with a teacher. Others think that it is always better to have a teacher. Which view do you prefer?

Secondly, **teachers intrinsically motivate students to keep studying subjects.** By themselves, ~~they~~ students can lose ~~their~~ interest ~~on~~ in their studies, unless the subjects are **directly related to their daily lives.** However, **in school,** teachers will stimulate students' interest in class by giving ~~today's~~ the **aim of the class** and various educational materials. **For example,** before a speaking activity, a teacher can play a recorded dialogue as a listening material ~~where~~ in which native English speakers are having a conversation about ~~some~~ a topic, then s/he will say to the students, "later this class, you can communicate this topic in native-like intonation just like the people in the ~~tape~~ **dialogue.**"

- This is a well-written and clear topic sentence that controls the paragraph. I expect to now read specific details about <u>how</u> teachers motivate students to keep studying.

- Maybe it would be better to state something about the student's interests rather than 'daily life.' Eating and washing are part of our daily lives.

- Just be careful, as the question mentions 'teachers,' not 'schools.' It is possible to have a teacher at home for instance.

- A well-chosen example, but make sure you directly relate the example to 'how a teacher motivates students to <u>keep</u> studying.'

- Better to keep the same word as you originally used to describe the recording in order to avoid confusion.

- The paragraph is missing a concluding sentence.

Here is how the marker tried to improve this paragraph:

Secondly, teachers intrinsically motivate students to keep studying subjects. By trying to study by themselves, students can easily lose their interest in their studies even if they like the subject. However, teachers can stimulate interest in study by making the lessons more varied and more interesting; they can give the aim of the class and can provide fun educational materials. For example, before a speaking activity, a teacher can play a recorded dialogue as a listening material in which native English speakers are having a conversation, then he/she can role-play with the student using the dialogue as a framework. This type of assistance provided by a teacher fundamentally makes acquiring knowledge more fun and interesting, which in turn helps students to continue learning.

Essential Skills

Skill A: Writing topic sentences

Remember, each paragraph should only contain one idea or topic, so a topic sentence must also only contain one idea. A topic sentence should summarize what the paragraph will be about, it must control the paragraph so the reader knows what to expect to read, and it must not contain too much specific detail.

Exercise 3c

Choose the best topic sentence. There is an explanation about the correct answer in the answer key at the back of the book.

❶ a. Firstly, Germany has one of the most accessible university systems in the world.

   b. Firstly, some universities in Germany offer free tuition, and make no distinction between international and domestic students so Germany has a great university system.

❷ a. The best attributes a person can have is to be hardworking and trustworthy.

   b. The best attribute a person can have is to be hardworking.

❸ a. Poor sanitation is one explanation for the rise in infant mortality rates.

   b. For example, in some countries infants do not have access to clean water and they often live too close to unhygienic sewage facilities.

Read the following thesis statements. Write a topic sentence using the highlighted argument/statement. A sample answer is provided in the answer key at the back of the book.

> **Thesis statement:**
> The world of fashion changed dramatically in the 1920s. Women discarded restrictive corsets and enjoyed more freedom in their attire, and men abandoned formal wear in favour of sports clothes. We can see the influence of 1920s fashion in the more casual style of clothing worn today.

Topic sentence:

....

....

....

2

> **Thesis statement:**
> While downsizing can give some short-term benefits to a company, in the long-term downsizing is not an effective business strategy as it de-motivates staff and decreases production capacity.

Topic sentence:

....

....

....

3

Thesis statement:
The fact that food is now much easier to prepare than it was in the past has definitely improved people's lives; firstly, people have more free time and secondly, they can try to cook more exotic and delicious dishes.

Topic sentence:

....

....

....

Skill B: Writing concluding sentences

Remember, a concluding sentence must not contain any new information, it should not just repeat what has already been written, and it should relate directly to your topic sentence.

Exercise 3e

Read the following topic sentences and the supporting detail that would be in a paragraph. Then, write a concluding sentence. Refer to the two main types of concluding sentence on page 49 to help with this exercise. A sample answer is provided in the answer key at the back of the book.

Topic sentence:

Many people simply return to their original weight as soon as they stop their diet.

Detail 1: **diets are not combined with an exercise program**

Detail 2: **people do not change the type or quantity of food they consume**

Concluding sentence – type 1 (paraphrase + main details):

....

....

....

❷

Topic sentence:
Global warming is causing the sea level to rise.
Detail 1: recent research has shown the sea has risen significantly in the last decade
Detail 2: further research has shown that the Antarctic sea glaciers are melting faster than predicted due to the hole in the ozone layer

Concluding sentence – **type 1 (paraphrase + main details):**

....

....

....

❸

Topic sentence:
Firstly, advertisements need to be more closely regulated.
Detail 1: too easy to make false claims that can be misleading
Detail 2: vulnerable people can be adversely influenced

Concluding sentence – **type 2 (position / opinion):**

....

....

....

Further Practice

These are the same questions to which you wrote an introduction in Unit 2. Using your thesis statements from Unit 2, Further Practice, write two topic sentences and two concluding sentences for each question. Use this checklist to evaluate each of your topic sentences and concluding sentences.

Topic sentence	YES	NO
Is the topic sentence directly related to one of the arguments/ points in the thesis statement?		
Is the topic sentence a summary of what the paragraph will be about?		
Does it control the paragraph?		
Has it excluded details?		
Concluding sentence	**YES**	**NO**
Is the concluding sentence directly related to the topic sentence?		
Does it either rephrase the topic sentence without adding new information, or give a definitive opinion / explanation?		
Does it avoid simply re-writing what has already been stated?		

❶ There should be more boys-only and more girls-only schools. Do you agree or disagree?

Topic sentence 1:

....

....

....

Concluding sentence 1:

....

....

....

Topic sentence 2:

....

....

....

Concluding sentence 2:

....

....

....

2 **How do movies or television influence people's behavior? Use reasons and specific examples to support your answer.**

Topic sentence 1:

....

....

....

Concluding sentence 1:

....

....

....

Topic sentence 2:

....

....

....

Concluding sentence 2:

....

....

....

3 **Compare and contrast knowledge gained from experience with knowledge gained from books.**

Topic sentence 1:

....

....

....

Concluding sentence 1:

....

....

....

Topic sentence 2:

....

....

....

Concluding sentence 2:

....

....

....

Writing Focus

Once you have written your topic sentence you must add the detail to the paragraph and include the appropriate amount of support for your position or statement.

What comes after the topic sentence?

▶ First, you must expand and reinforce your topic sentence.

▶ You must then provide support to validate your position or argument.

▶ Everything you write in the paragraph must be directly related to the topic sentence.

How do I "expand and reinforce" my topic sentence?

▶ First, expand by adding details and relevant information about the topic.

▶ Second, reinforce your position or argument by stating your position (opinion, agree/disagree, or preference essays) or by providing more facts (cause and effect, compare and contrast essays, or advantages/disadvantages essays).

How do I "validate" my position or argument?

▶ Use a personal experience, or a piece of research, a quotation, a well-known/easily verifiable factual statement. The validation must be directly relevant and must be detailed enough to support your point.

What comes after the validation?

▶ Finish each paragraph with a concluding sentence (See Unit 3).

Let's recap what each paragraph must do:

▶ It must tell the reader the one point of the paragraph (Topic sentence + expand/reinforce).

▶ It must show the reader–by using evidence or examples–how or why your point is valid (Validate + Concluding sentence).

▶ It must directly relate to the thesis statement.

Let's *analyze* a paragraph:

This is the same topic sentence you analyzed in Unit 3. Assume the question has asked you to discuss how cosmetic companies sell their products, and also to give your opinion.

(A) A cosmetics company sells its products by appealing to a person's desire to look younger.

(B) From bathing in milk to pressing poppy petals onto their lips, people have always searched for ways to maintain a youthful appearance, and this natural human desire forms the basis of cosmetic companies' marketing strategies.

(C) However, they use some unethical methods in order to tempt people into buying their creams and lotions, such as employing pretty models and using photo editing tools to make these models look younger than they actually are.

(D) For example, in the UK a TV advertisement was banned because it showed 'before and after' pictures of models using a skin care cream. However, the pictures taken after they had used the cream were digitally enhanced and therefore misleading.

(E) The techniques often used by a cosmetic company to sell its creams and treatments amount to false advertising and are immoral.

A The topic sentence tells the reader exactly what the paragraph will be about.

B The first sentence after the topic sentence expands the topic sentence and adds some background information.

C The second sentence after the topic sentence reinforces your position and adds the reasons for your opinion (unethical because of pretty models and photo editing).

D Then, you must validate your position. In academic writing you would need to cite the source of this example (see Unit 9).

E The concluding sentence summarizes your position.

Korean students of English wrote the following paragraphs. Use the checklist below each topic sentence and compare your answers with those in the answer key at the back of the book.

Model 1

Moreover, the Internet became alternative part of human life. The cyber space the Internet created is a place where everybody is treated equal. Plus, the Internet provides everyone a chance to be more involved into categories that one pursues to learn. This can be best illustrated by disabled working in the cyber space. Even though disabled's physical condition keeps them from working like others do, the Internet provides equal opportunity.

Paragraph	YES	NO
Does the paragraph contain only one position or argument?		
Is there a strong topic sentence?		
Is the topic sentence 'expanded and explained' in the next few sentences?		
Is the position or opinion 'reinforced'?		
Is there sufficient 'validation' of the position or argument?		
Is there a strong concluding sentence?		

Model 2

Firstly, by saving money, it helps me to succeed. Since the society is highly competitive. As are thousands of rivals that one must prevail over in the competitive job market, possessing superior saving money skills is required for succeed. By saving money, my cousin was able to buy a new shop and he earned a lot of money. So, I think to save money is important that for one to succeed. Saving money helpful to succeed.

Paragraph	YES	NO
Does the paragraph contain only one position or argument?		
Is there a strong topic sentence?		
Is the topic sentence 'expanded and explained' in the next few sentences?		
Is the position or opinion 'reinforced'?		
Is there sufficient 'validation' of the position or argument?		
Is there a strong concluding sentence?		

Real Essays

In this section we will review a paragraph written by a Korean student of English.

step 1 First, read the paragraph and highlight parts that could be improved. There is a note section at the end of the paragraph for you to write your ideas and comments.

Question: Do you agree or disagree with the following statement. People should read only non-fiction books.

Some people believe that reading fiction books would not have any benefits for people. They believe fiction books is just one of the entertainments such as video games. Therefore, in their belief, people who like to read fiction books would think less. However, this is not true. Fiction books can prompt people to think creatively. People can learn many things through these fiction books. For instance, if some one prefers fiction books, he or she can realize how to think and how to develop diverse standing out production such as robots by reading fiction books. Eventually, in doing so, the person can become scientists after someday. People can wide a range of thinking through the scientific fictional books. Therefore, the effect of fiction books should be positive not only for whole of humanity but also personality.

Your notes:

....

....

....

step 2 Here are some comments made by the marker of this paragraph. Compare the marker's comments with the items you found.

Marker's Comments

Question: Do you agree or disagree with the following statement. People should read only non-fiction books.

Some people believe that reading fiction books would not have any benefits ~~for people~~. They believe fiction books ~~is~~ are just ~~a one~~ type of ~~the~~ entertainments, ~~such as~~ just like video games. Therefore, in their belief, people who like to read fiction books would think less. However, this is not true. Fiction books can prompt people to think creatively. People can learn many things through these fiction books. For instance, if ~~some one~~ someone prefers fiction books, he or she can realize how to think and how to develop diverse standing out production such as robots by reading fiction books. Eventually, in doing so, the person ~~can~~ might become a scientists ~~after~~ someday. People can experience a wide ~~a~~ range of thinking through the scientific fictional books. Therefore, the effect of fiction books ~~should~~ can be positive not only for ~~the~~ whole of humanity but also for a person's personality.

- There are a lot of short sentences in this paragraph. Think how these could be combined.

- Well done, you have expanded the topic sentence adequately – there is a direct link between 'no benefits' and 'thinking less.'

- Perhaps these sentences could also be combined.

- This is a little awkward. I think you mean that 'by reading fiction people may be inspired to create fantastic products such as robots.'

- 'Scientific' means 'to be based on the principles of science.' The correct phrase for this genre is 'science fiction' books.

- 'Should' is mostly used to express suggestions or advice. 'Can' is a better word to express possibility.

Here is how the marker tried to improve this paragraph:

Some people believe that reading fiction has no real benefit. They think that fiction books are just a form of entertainment, just like a video game, and that nothing can be learned from them. However, this is not true. Reading fiction prompts people's imaginations, helps them to think creatively, and can even inspire them to become scientists and inventors. For instance, by reading fiction people can be exposed to a wide range of diverse topics that they would not normally encounter in their day-to-day lives, and this can increase their capability to think about things in a new and open manner. Therefore, reading fiction can be positive for an individual and, if it helps a person become innovative and inventive, it can even benefit the whole of society.

Essential Skills

Skill A: Transitions

Transition words and phrases are used to show connections in your writing. They are a very important component of writing, and you need to know how to use transitions correctly to be able to write good paragraphs.

For example, imagine you heard this sentence: "You have won the lottery..." Would you prefer the next word to be 'however' or would you prefer the next word to be 'therefore.' Both of these words are transitions, and they signal to the reader what will come next (the connection) in the sentence:

> You have won the lottery, **however**, so have one million other people.
> You have won the lottery, **therefore** you can retire immediately.

Some key transition words and phrases are:

To introduce more points
equally important, firstly (secondly, etc.), furthermore, in addition, also, another, moreover, next, lastly, finally

To introduce examples and supporting details
for example, for instance, to illustrate, in fact, specifically, that is, as seen in

To compare
in a similar way, similarly, likewise, also, in the same manner

To contrast
although, despite, even though, however, in contrast, in spite of, nevertheless, on the contrary, on the other hand, but, conversely

To show cause and effect
because, consequently, for this reason, hence, as a result, thus, due to, therefore, if, so, since

To acknowledge the other viewpoint before stating your viewpoint

whereas, granted that, even though, though, while, although

To summarize

in conclusion, in summary, on the whole, therefore, to sum up, in short, for the reasons illustrated

You must make sure you use transitions between the different parts within a paragraph (such as using 'for instance' to introduce your validation), and you must use transitions between the paragraphs (such as 'In conclusion' to begin the conclusion).

Fill in the blanks by choosing an appropriate transition. Answers are provided in the answer key at the back of this book.

❶ The swimming pool became dirty _____ nobody cleaned it.

❷ _____ exercise is good for me, I prefer watching TV.

❸ Acid rain is harmful to the environment. _____ , deforestation is also bad for the planet.

❹ Too much cultural diversity in a city can cause challenges. _____ , there are some schools in London that have to provide learning material in five or more languages.

❺ Environmental conditions in some countries are stable, _____ other countries suffer from all kinds of environmental problems.

❻ Video games are detrimental to a child's development. Firstly, they take too much of a child's time, and _____ they have very little educational merit.

Skill B: Validating your point or argument

After you have 'expanded and reinforced' your topic sentence you must validate your point or argument. For TOEFL or IELTS examinations you can provide examples from personal experience or use well-known facts. If you were writing academically you would need to cite research correctly (See Unit 9).

You must make sure your validation is directly relevant, it must be detailed enough to support your point, and if it is a piece of research or a fact it must be verifiable (which means the reader should be able to find the information you have used by himself or herself if he or she wanted to).

The most common ways to validate are:
▶ a personal experience: For instance, in my neighbourhood everybody knows the police officers, and this has helped create a greater sense of community.
▶ a piece of research: In fact, a recent research paper published by the *British Medical Journal* proved the link between poor gum health and heart disease.
▶ a quotation: This point is illustrated effectively by James E. Burke when he said, "We don't grow unless we take risks. Any successful company is riddled with failures."
▶ a well-known or easily verifiable factual statement: And as seen by the fact that even just leaving the water running while brushing your teeth can use up to 4 gallons of water in a minute, water preservation is extremely important.

Choose the best validation for each of the following topic sentences. There is an explanation about the correct answer in the answer key at the back of the book.

❶ **For non-native speakers, studying English in an English speaking country can diminish a person's confidence.**

 a. For example, being exposed to English every day can be confusing and can lead to a lack of confidence.

 b. For example, my older sister went to America to study English last summer but the whole experience was overwhelming. She felt afraid to speak to native speakers and was ashamed about her pronunciation.

❷ **The best way to improve young people's health would be to ban junk food.**

 a. In fact, 47 million customers globally are served every day by just one of the famous American fast food chains.

 b. As can be seen from research into childhood obesity, junk food accounts for over half of a young person's weekly intake of sugar and harmful fats.

❸ **Women should have an equal role alongside men in the police force.**

 a. In fact, my mother is a policewoman and she has been promoted twice in the last five years.

 b. In fact, a recent survey supports this assertion. It was shown that communication skills are considered the greatest asset of a police officer, and most people answered that women have better communication skills than men.

Use the given information and write a few sentences to <u>validate</u> the position or argument. Make sure you use an appropriate transition word or phrase. An example answer is provided in the answer key at the back of the book.

1

Topic sentence:

Marriage is not considered as important as it was in the past. ....

Validation:

Information to use for validation:
In 1996 10% of marriages ended in divorce; in 2008 33% of marriages ended in divorce. Source: Someland Bureau of Facts, 2010

....

....

....

....

2

Topic sentence:

Embracing change is a sign of maturity.

Validation:

Information to use for validation:
A wise man changes his mind, but a fool never will.
Spanish proverb

....

....

....

....

3

Topic sentence:

Some people are attracted to dangerous sports because this type of sport allows them to escape the routine of their day-to-day lives.

Validation:

Information to use for validation:
Father works in a factory performing a boring job.
Every weekend he goes scuba diving.

....

....

....

....

Further Practice

These are the same questions to which you wrote an introduction in Unit 2 and topic/concluding sentences in Unit 3. Using your topic and concluding sentences from Unit 3, write <u>two complete body paragraphs for each question</u>. Use this checklist to evaluate your paragraphs.

Paragraph	YES	NO
Do the paragraphs contain only one position or argument?		
Does each paragraph have a strong topic sentence?		
Is the topic sentence 'expanded and explained' in the next few sentences of each paragraph?		
Is the position or opinion 'reinforced' in each paragraph?		
Is there sufficient 'validation' of the position or argument in each paragraph?		
Does each paragraph have a strong concluding sentence?		

1 **There should be more boys-only and more girls-only schools. Do you agree or disagree?**

Body paragraph 1:

_____

_____

_____

_____

_____

Body paragraph 2:

_____

_____

_____

_____

_____

❷ How do movies or television influence people's behavior? Use reasons and specific examples to support your answer.

Body paragraph 1:

Body paragraph 2:

❸ Compare and contrast knowledge gained from experience with knowledge gained from books.

Body paragraph 1:

Body paragraph 2:

Writing Focus

The conclusion is the last thing that is seen by your reader. It is your last chance to make a good impression and convince the reader that you have written a good essay.

What must a conclusion do?

▶ It must finish the essay by completely and directly answering the question.
▶ It should paraphrase the thesis statement / restate the main points made in the essay, and this must be done in a new and innovative way.
▶ It should not just repeat what has already been said in the introduction and body paragraphs.
▶ It must not focus on minor points.
▶ It must not introduce any new ideas, topics or arguments.
▶ It must be brief and concise.

How do I structure a conclusion?

▶ First, use a clear 'conclusion transition.'

<u>Conclusion transitions:</u>
in conclusion, in summary, on the whole, therefore, to sum up, in short, for the reasons illustrated

▶ Second, directly answer the question.

▶ Third, paraphrase your thesis statement / restate the main points of the essay.

▶ Lastly, write a final comment.

What is a final comment?

▶ A good conclusion will fully answer the question and a 'final comment' helps to reinforce the message of your essay. Depending on the type of essay you are writing a final comment could be:

• A response to the background information or hook in the introduction.

• A suggestion or solution to a problem.

• A general statement relevant to your position on the topic.

• A clever way to confirm your opinion or preference.

• Occasionally, a question for the reader to ponder.

Let's *analyze* **a conclusion:**

Q: A university should give the same amount of money to its art department as it gives to its English department. Do you agree or disagree?

(A) Therefore, it is imperative that art departments receive equal funding to English departments.

(B) Without adequate finances a university's art department cannot nurture the talented artists of the future, and it cannot attract the best teaching staff.

(C) We may never find the next Da Vinci or the next Michelangelo if we neglect to support university art departments.

(A) The first sentence directly answers the question and has a clear conclusion transition. It clearly shows that it agrees with the statement, even though it does not explicitly say 'I agree...'

(B) This part paraphrases the arguments from a thesis statement.

(C) This is the **final comment.** In this case it reinforces the message of the essay by making a statement relevant to the writer's position on the topic.

Korean students of English wrote the following conclusions. Use the checklist to evaluate the conclusions. Compare your answers with those in the answer key at the back of the book.

Q: Some people think they can learn better by themselves than with a teacher. Others think that it is always better to have a teacher. Which view do you prefer?

In conclusion, the teacher plays critical roles for the students to improve and develop their English abilities in aspects of cognitive and affective aspects, so they can more effectively learn English for their teacher.

	YES	NO
Is there a clear 'conclusion transition'?		
Does the first sentence directly answer the question?		
Does the conclusion state the main arguments that support the writer's position on the topic?		
Does the conclusion contain a final comment?		

2

Q: Some people think they can learn better by themselves than with a teacher. Others think that it is always better to have a teacher. Which view do you prefer?

Therefore, it is better to study with teachers because they can be willing to respond to students' doubts on the subjects. Additionally, they will draw students' participation in class by giving the aim of the class and various resources, and keep the students' motivation high.

	YES	NO
Is there a clear 'conclusion transition'?		
Does the first sentence directly answer the question?		
Does the conclusion state the main arguments that support the writer's position on the topic?		
Does the conclusion contain a final comment?		

Real Essays

In this section we will review a conclusion written by a Korean student of English.

step 1 Read through the student's conclusion and highlight parts that could be improved. There is a note section at the end of the essay for you to write your ideas and comments.

Question: Only the most intelligent and hard-working students should be allowed to attend university. Do you agree or disagree with this statement?

For the reasons illustrated above, I believe that colleges and universities have gone through a hard decision; limiting students entering higher education. It is evident that this choice was made because it would be much more beneficial to the school and to the students. To sum up, I think we should stop complaining about how we can't enter any universities we want, but improve our skills to be fit for these schools.

Your notes:

....

....

....

....

step 2 Here are some comments made by the marker of this conclusion. Compare the marker's comments with the items you found.

Question: Only the most intelligent and hardworking students should be allowed to attend university. Do you agree or disagree with this statement?

For the reasons illustrated above, ~~I be-lieve that~~ colleges and universities have ~~gone through~~ a hard decision; limiting the number of students entering higher education. It is evident that this choice was made because it would be much more beneficial to the school and to the students. To sum up, I think we should stop complaining about how we ~~can't~~ cannot enter ~~any universities we want~~ university, ~~but rather~~ we should improve our skills to be fit for these schools.

 Marker's Comments

- Even in an 'agree/disagree' question it is better to use the third person. These words could be deleted: '...above, colleges and...'

- Better as 'taken.'

- The conclusion should restate the exact reasons/arguments made in the thesis statement and topic sentences. This is too general.

- This is the second 'conclusion transition' – only use one.

- Do not use contractions.

step 3 Here is how the marker tried to improve this conclusion:

For the reasons illustrated, it is proper that universities have taken the decision to only admit the best students. The university can provide lessons targeted at the right academic level, and students can study with peers of equal ability to themselves. People should stop complaining about the admission criteria of universities, and instead they should improve their skills to be fit for higher education.

Essential Skills

<u>Skill A: Avoiding common errors in your conclusions</u>

Common errors in conclusions include:
- ▶ not directly answering the question
- ▶ not including a final comment
- ▶ adding new information, ideas or arguments
- ▶ making the conclusion too long
- ▶ adding minor details and repeating what has already been mentioned in the body paragraphs.

Exercise 5b

Try to find the errors in the following conclusions. See the answer key at the back of the book for explanations.

Q: Do artists contribute more to our society than scientists?

To sum up, an artist is a person who creates great sculpture, fantastic paintings, wonderful poems or interesting novels. In addition to the points already mentioned in the essay, artists also help us to forget about our day-to-day lives and they should receive a very high salary for what they do. Without art, what type of world would we live in?

Your notes:

....

....

....

....

2

Q: Do artists contribute more to our society than scientists?

In conclusion, scientists benefit society far more than artists. Art can help people to relax and become more creative. People can visit museums after a hard day at work, and artists show people how to see everyday things in new ways. Therefore artists make a positive contribution to society. However, it is scientists who develop the medicines people need to live more comfortable lives. Scientists also develop the technology that makes people's lives convenient and exciting, especially at work where technology has revolutionised the way people complete their duties.

Your notes:

....

....

....

....

Skill B: Answering the question and restating your points/arguments in your conclusion

Should I just paraphrase my thesis statement?

▶ Your first sentence should directly answer the question. Then make sure your conclusion restates the main arguments of your essay, and if you have written a good thesis statement you can do this by paraphrasing your thesis statement. You should try to present the information in a new and innovative way.

Let's *analyze* an example of paraphrasing a thesis statement for your conclusion:

Thesis statement:
Modern life has destroyed communication amongst family members. People spend more time watching TV than conversing, and they are too busy to eat dinner with their family.

Paraphrase for conclusion:
In conclusion, family members do not talk together as much as they did in the past. Family meals are not prioritized over other aspects of life, and talking with each other has been replaced by staring at the TV in silence.

In the paraphrase, the message remains the same as in the thesis statement, but the language and structure are different.

Read each question and introduction, and then:
- *write the first sentence of the conclusion to directly answer the question. Make sure you use a clear conclusion transition*
- *paraphrase the thesis statement*

1

Q: Some people like doing work by hand. Others prefer using machines. Which do you prefer?

Introduction:

These days there are machines for everything. From cooking an egg to removing wallpaper, there is a machine that can help. But while machines have many obvious benefits, doing work by hand is better. When people make something by hand they feel a sense of achievement in completing something by themselves, and it is only by doing something by hand that a person can be sure the work will be done correctly.

First sentence of the conclusion to answer the question:	
Paraphrase of the thesis statement:	

2

Q: In many countries, obesity levels in children are increasing. Explain why this is happening and what the implications are.

Introduction:

All around the world a disease is rapidly spreading. It is not a virus and it is not contagious, but it can be deadly. The prevalence of childhood obesity is increasing, and there are two main causes and consequences. Children eat too much sugar and too much fat, leading to weight gain and diseases such as diabetes. Also, children spend too much time indoors watching TV or playing on the computer, and therefore they do not get the exercise they need in order to maintain a healthy weight.

First sentence of the conclusion to answer the question:	
Paraphrase of the thesis statement:	

Further Practice

These are the same questions you have answered in Units 2, 3 and 4. Refer to your answers in those units and write an appropriate and complete <u>conclusion</u>. Use this checklist to evaluate each conclusion.

	YES	NO
First section		
Is there a clear 'conclusion transition'?		
Does the first sentence directly answer the question?		
Second section		
Does the conclusion state the main arguments that support the writer's position on the topic?		
Third section		
Does the conclusion contain a final comment?		

1 **There should be more boys-only and more girls-only schools. Do you agree or disagree?**

2 How do movies or television influence people's behavior? Use reasons and specific examples to support your answer.

3 Compare and contrast knowledge gained from experience with knowledge gained from books.

Section

2

Writing Skills

Section

2

Writing Skills

Unit 6 Writing Better Sentences

Writing Focus

In any communication the goal is to make sure that you are fully and completely understood. There are three key questions that you should always ask yourself when you are writing:

1 – Is this exactly what I mean?
2 – Is this easy for the reader to understand?
3 – Can I make this sentence shorter and clearer?

There are some key skills that will help you with these questions and enable you to write clear and concise sentences:

principle 1 Learn collocations

Using the correct word is obviously extremely important, and possessing a large vocabulary will enable you to write more interesting and concise essays. However, many people learn words but do not learn how to use them correctly and naturally. One of the best ways to learn how to write naturally is to learn collocations.

Words that often come together in a set pattern are called collocations. Learning collocations is a very good way to ensure your sentences are grammatically correct and clearly composed.

For example, we always 'take a picture' rather than 'make a picture,' and we have 'a pack of playing cards' rather than 'a box of playing cards.'

Choose the correct collocation and write a sentence. Sample answers are in the answer key at the back of the book.

1 take a rest / do a rest

....

2 a bar of chocolate / a block of chocolate

....

3 get out of time / run out of time

....

4 go abroad / go to abroad

....

5 grab an agreement / reach an agreement

....

Do not use colloquial words and phrases

A colloquialism is a word or phrase that is informal and mostly used in speaking rather than writing. For instance, 'kids,' 'kid around' and 'No kidding' are often used in speech, but are better written as 'children,' 'play jokingly' and 'I cannot believe it.'

Exercise 6b

Try to write a more appropriate phrase for each of these colloquialisms.

❶ Children should not **hang out** with people much older than them.

....

❷ I **got into** rock music while I was at university.

....

❸ The comedian was **cool**, but his last joke **bombed**.

....

❹ Employees often **mess up** at work.

....

❺ Stress must not **get the better of** you.

....

Keep it simple

Do not try to be too clever with your vocabulary. Of course, it is great to use academic and 'intelligent-sounding' words to demonstrate your ability to use English, but never compromise on clarity. Look at these examples:

☹ Appropriately employ accurate vocabulary in order to impart the desired communiqué.

☺ Use the correct word in the correct way to say the correct thing.

☹ The propensity of politicians to avoid directly answering questions habitually initiates misapprehension.

☺ Often politicians do not actually answer the question, so people cannot understand what they mean.

Rewrite each sentence to make it clearer. Sample answers are in the answer key at the back of the book.

1 The intake of excessive disagreeable nutrients facilitates the onset of obesity.

....

....

2 Adhering to the latest fashion vogue invariably distracts a person from more important pursuits, such as study and such forth.

....

....

3 Continuously watching movies prohibits a person from learning the pre-requisite social skills needed in all circumstances.

....

....

Avoid redundancy

Redundancy just means using words or phrases that are repeated and/or not necessary. There are two main types of redundancy in writing:

1) Often a writer will add words or phrases that do not add any information to a sentence. For instance:

☺ The vote was completely unanimous.
☺ The vote was unanimous.
   ▶ The word 'unanimous' means 'done by everybody,' so the word 'completely' does not add any more information.

☺ A total of one hundred people took part in the vote.
☺ One hundred people took part in the vote.
   ▶ 'A total of' does not add information. We know 100 people voted if we read either sentence.

☺ Everybody cooperated together.
☺ Everybody cooperated.
   ▶ It is impossible to cooperate alone, so 'together' is redundant.

2) Secondly, whole sentences are sometimes added that simply repeat what has already been written. For instance:

☺ A business has a moral obligation to ensure that it does not pollute the environment. Environmental pollution is a big problem these days and a business should have ethics that ensure it does not cause pollution.

☺ Pollution is a big problem these days, and a business has a moral obligation to ensure that it does not pollute the environment.

Always review your sentences to make sure that every word and phrase is absolutely necessary. If you remove a word or phrase from a sentence and the meaning stays the same, the piece you removed is redundant.

Look at these passages written by Korean students of English and highlight the redundant parts. The answers are in the answer key at the back of the book.

1 The age 20 to 25 will be the very busiest time in the life, it is much busier than other times of life such as 15-19. But among the things they should do, the most absolute important thing that they should do is to study lessons in the college. College is the first and maybe the last place that one can choose themselves the class that one want to study. The education in the college can decide one's field or career. Meaning, the college can decide one's future life.

2 Second, the government spend a lot of money to educate students. Students have to go to school until middle school. While students go to middle school, government try to make good environment to study and make comfortable to study in the schools, it spends a lot of money.

principle 5 Use better verbs and nouns

Using better verbs and nouns makes your writing concise, and often even eliminates the need to use adjectives and adverbs. Look at the following examples:

He ran to get the bus.
The water ran down the hill.
A book about climbing mountains.

In each sentence, you could add adjectives or adverbs to provide more information:

He ran quickly to get the bus.
The water ran rapidly down the hill.
A fictional book about climbing mountains.

But by using stronger verbs or nouns in your writing you can make your sentences more concise and reduce the number of words you use:

He sprinted to get the bus.
The water poured down the hill.
A novel about climbing mountains.

Try to rewrite these sentences using better verbs and nouns. Sample answers are in the answer key at the back of the book.

❶ Knowledge got from books is better than knowledge got from experience.

....

❷ At sports stadiums people are always sat too close together.

....

❸ Too often, a teacher tells off a student for something unimportant.

....

A <u>cliché</u> is a phrase that has been used so many times it has become worn out and unsuitable for writing. Often, the meaning of a cliché is not completely understood and therefore you should avoid including them in your writing. Some example clichés are:

Last but not least
☹ Last but not least, the government should...
☺ Equally important is that the government should....

Take the bull by the horns
☹ The government must take the bull by the horns and...
☺ The government must confront this issue and....

Cool, calm and collected
☹ The president's demeanor was cool, calm and collected.
☺ The president was calm and confident.

A <u>euphemism</u> is a word or phrase that is used instead of a word or phrase that might be considered too harsh or inappropriate. Used correctly, euphemisms can be effective in reducing the impact of a statement, and they are often used in difficult personal situations. However, the exact meaning of a euphemism is often unclear, and they should be avoided in essay writing. Some example euphemisms are:

'downsizing,' 'slimming down' or 'restructuring' to mean redundancy
'handy sized' or 'fun-sized' to mean small
'the call of nature' to mean to go to the bathroom

Rewrite this passage, changing all of the clichés and euphemisms.
A sample answer is in the answer key at the back of the book.

Lucy's enforced contract termination was a crying shame. Her strategic withdrawal from the board of directors came as a crushing blow to her, especially as her mother had recently passed away. She left the rat race and went to live in the countryside. Many of her friends were green with envy about her new lifestyle, but she soon became sick and tired of it.

....

....

....

....

....

....

....

....

principle 7 Use fewer words to say the same thing

Unnecessarily long phrases are often written just because a phrase has been learned or is in common use. For instance:

☹ Due to the fact that global warming...
☺ Because global warming...
▶ 'due to the fact that' just means 'because.'

☹ In the event that the government loses the election...
☺ If the government loses the election...
▶ 'in the event that' just means 'if.'

Occasionally using a well-known phrase can make your writing more varied and interesting. However, to write concise sentences try to avoid using them too often.

Rewrite these sentences using fewer words. Sample answers are in the answer key at the back of the book.

1 During the course of the interview it became apparent to me that I would not be offered the position.

....

....

2 The Principal came to the conclusion that the school should reduce the total number of teachers it employed.

....

....

3 In the process of writing an essay a student can learn about a great number of different things.

....

....

Make sure your English flows.

English is not a series of short sentences. It should flow naturally. Many people write lots of short sentences. They should really try to use conjunctions a bit more.

Or....

English is not a series of short sentences; instead it should flow naturally. Many people write lots of short sentences, but they should really try to use conjunctions a bit more.

Conjunctions are the words that link other words, phrases or clauses. If you use them to ensure that your writing contains a variety of sentence structures and lengths, your writing will become more natural. The most common conjunctions are:

Type of conjunction	Examples
Coordinating	and, for, but, or, so, yet, nor
Subordinating	because, since, although, while, even though, even if, whereas, though, so that, in that, in order that, if, unless, provided that

A **coordinating conjunction** joins words, phrases or clauses that are equally important. For instance:

A new university in the town will lead to noise pollution **and** traffic congestion.

In this sentence the writer wants to emphasize that noise pollution and traffic congestion are two, equally important, consequences of the new university.

A **subordinating conjunction** joins words, phrases or clauses where one idea is more important than the other. For instance:

A new university in the town will lead to noise pollution **because of** traffic congestion.

Here, the writer wants to emphasize noise pollution as the main idea, while traffic congestion is a supporting reason.

Make this passage more natural by using conjunctions and changing a few words. A sample answer is in the answer key at the back of the book.

> People should demonstrate more. A government needs to understand that people really do care. People need to protest. The government must have incentive to change. Throughout history there are examples where public protest has led to change. For example, Martin Luther King. He led protests about civil rights. America is now a very different place.

....

....

....

....

....

....

....

....

Note: There are some more exercises using conjunctions in Unit 7 – Common Errors.

Further Practice

These passages were written by Korean students of English. Try to rewrite them more clearly and concisely using the skills you have covered in this unit.

1

> More and more, according to the progress in mobile phone technology, upgrading of mobile phone in new is very diverse and relevant. When upgrading, a new mobile phone's not just used for contact each other but also the phone is material for other things like Internet.

....

....

....

2

> In conclusion, to wedge the learning in life, the most important way is the personal experience by doing directly, because it facilitates internalization and cause a broader knowledge, so they develop the people's growth.

....

....

....

Writing Focus

This chapter looks at some of the most common errors made by Korean students of English.

1. Pronouns

A pronoun replaces a noun so that you do not need to repeat the noun over and over again. If pronouns are used correctly, they make your writing much more natural.

There are many different types of pronoun. Some of the most commonly used pronouns are:

> The personal pronouns for people are:
> **I, you, he, she, we, they, me, him, her, us, their and them**
>
> The personal pronouns for things are:
> **it, they, them**

The two most common errors in using pronouns are:

1) Not referring clearly to a specific noun:

☺ The car is very fast. *It* has a powerful engine.
▶ The pronoun 'It' obviously refers to the noun 'car.'

☺ Jamie told Steve that *his* car was too slow.

▶ In this sentence we do not know whether the pronoun 'his' refers to Jamie's car or Steve's car. This sentence needs to be written as "Jamie told Steve that *his own* car was too slow." We now know that Jamie is referring to his own car, and not Steve's car.

☺ I called the shop and spoke to an assistant. *They* said *they* did not have any noodles in stock.

▶ In this sentence the pronoun 'they' is used twice, but it is used to mean two different things. The first 'they' refers to the assistant, but the second 'they' is referring to the shop.

2) Not agreeing in number (singular/plural) or person (first person, third person, etc.)

☺ I called the shop and spoke to an assistant. *They* said *they* did not have any noodles in stock.

▶ This is the same sentence as in the third bullet point of part 1. In addition to not referring clearly to a specific noun, both uses of the pronoun 'they' are incorrect because the pronoun does not match in number. There is 'an assistant' which is singular, but the pronoun 'they' is plural. Also, a company or business is a singular entity, so the plural pronoun 'they' should not be used. This sentence needs to be written as "I called the shop and spoke to an assistant. *He* said *it* did not have any noodles in stock."

Note: If you do not know the gender of a singular person, you can write 'his or her' or 'he or she':

"If a student misses class, he or she will not get a good grade."

☺ If athletes do not train every day, *we* will not win any medals.

▶ This sentence has changed from third person (athletes) to the first person plural (we). This needs to be written as "If athletes do not train every day, *they* will not win any medals."

118

Correct the following pronoun errors. There may be more than one error in a sentence, and you may need to change the pronoun or use a noun rather than a pronoun.

❶ Each student must submit their homework by Friday.

....

....

❷ The business released their results last week, but they were very disappointing.

....

....

❸ The tree fell onto the house, but amazingly it was not damaged.

....

....

❹ I don't like my feet. It is unattractive.

....

....

5 If the children keep being naughty, you will be punished.

....

....

Exercise 7b

Read this passage written by a Korean student of English. Underline all the pronoun errors, and then rewrite the passage in the space provided. Check your answer using the answer key at the back of the book.

Another experience awaits students in other countries; you will live alone. From the exotic scenery and their lonely situation, they will appreciate the presence of them family and friends. Otherwise, they cannot easily recognize their importance no matter how an acquaintance exhorts the young adults to treat their family well. Therefore, when we listen to the lesson from his or her family and friends, they cannot truly be aware of it.

....

....

....

....

....

2. The article

A and An

▶ Use 'a' or 'an' when you are referring to one thing out of many things:

She has <u>a</u> dress. (We are referring to one dress even though there are many dresses.)

John is <u>a</u> nice person. (We are referring to one nice person even though there are many nice people.)

Can I have <u>a</u> drink please? (We are referring to one drink even though there are lots of drinks.)

It is <u>an</u> interesting idea. (We are referring to one idea even though there are lots of ideas.)

▶ 'a' is used when the pronunciation of the next word is a consonant <u>sound</u>, even if the word begins with a vowel. For instance, the words 'university' and 'unit' begin with a vowel, but the pronunciation is a consonant sound so they take the article 'a.'

▶ 'an' is used when the pronunciation of the next word is a vowel sound, even if the word begins with a consonant. For instance, the words 'honest' and 'hour' begin with a consonant, but the pronunciation is a vowel sound so they take the article 'an.'

The

▶ Use 'the' when you are referring to something that is the only one of something, or when you are referring to something you have already mentioned, or when you are referring to a type of something (with a single countable noun), or when to what you are referring is completely obvious:

Seoul is <u>the</u> capital city of Korea. (There is only one capital city of Korea.)

He is <u>the</u> nicest person in the office. (There can only be one 'nicest' person.)

Please pass me <u>the</u> drink. (There is only one drink available.)

Sarah has got a new bicycle. She will show you <u>the</u> bicycle tomorrow. (Sarah has one new bicycle that has been referred to previously.)

<u>The</u> elephant is a very big animal. ('The elephant' is a type of animal in this sentence; we are not talking about one specific elephant.)

It is on <u>the</u> door. (Even though there are many doors, it is obvious to which door you are referring.)

There are some other rules you need to know about using 'the':

▶ it is used with the following:
- musical instruments: the piano, the guitar, etc.
- the radio and the Internet
- names of seas, oceans, rivers: the Pacific ocean, the Han river
- names of countries that are republics, states or kingdoms: the United States of America, the United Kingdom
- names of countries that are plural: the Philippines, the Netherlands
- names of mountain ranges: the Himalayas, the Andes

▶ it is not used with the following:
- breakfast, lunch, dinner, next week/day/month/year/Monday etc,
- last week/day/month/year/Monday etc.
- names of countries or places that are not republics, states or kingdoms: China, Russia, Brazil, Tokyo, Paris
- places in towns and cities: Main Road, High Street, Times Square
- airports, universities, castles, palaces, stations, zoos: Incheon airport, Yale University, Leeds Castle, Buckingham Palace, Seoul Station, Berlin zoo

Exercise 7c

Fill in the blanks using either 'a,' 'an' or 'the':

In many countries .... birth rate is falling. If this trend continues it will have .... very big impact on society, because it will be harder for .... government to look after .... elderly. .... older person needs reasonable amount of income in order to live, but if there are less babies being born, eventually there will be .... smaller workforce who can pay ......taxes that can be used by .... government to provide .... pension to ....older generation. .... possible solution is to increase .... rate of tax, but this will be .... burden on .... workforce which could even lead to social unrest.

Check your answer using the answer key at the back of the book.

3. Fragments

If a sentence or clause is not complete, it is called a fragment. Fragments are sentences that end too quickly because there is something missing. The most common reasons for a fragment are that the sentence or clause:

▶ does not contain a subject
▶ does not contain a verb
▶ does not contain a helping verb with a verb + ing
▶ is not a complete thought and does not make sense by itself.

Fragments that do not contain a <u>subject</u>:
1. Drove from street to street looking for a restaurant.
2. <u>The hungry man</u> drove from street to street looking for a restaurant.

In the first sentence there is no subject, and therefore it is a fragment. In the second sentence we know <u>who</u> drove the car, which indicates a subject. Therefore it is not a fragment.

Fragments that do not contain a <u>verb</u>:
1. The lady really in the pool.
2. The lady really <u>swam</u> in the pool.

There is no verb in the first sentence, and therefore it is a fragment. In the second sentence we know what the lady <u>did</u> in the pool.

Fragments that do not contain a helping verb with a verb + ing:
1. The cleaner sweeping the floor.
2. The cleaner <u>is</u> sweeping the floor.

The 'ing' verb 'sweeping' needs the helping verb 'is' to make a complete sentence.

<u>'Helping verbs' to be used with verb + ing</u>
am, is, are, was, were, must, might, been, do, can, may, has, have, had, would, could, should, shall, will, does, did

There are two main ways to correct fragments that do not contain a helping verb with a verb + ing:

1. You can remove the 'ing' suffix and use the simple or perfect tense of the verb:
    · The cleaner <u>sweeps</u> the floor.
    · The cleaner <u>swept</u> the floor.
    · The cleaner <u>will sweep</u> the floor.
    · The cleaner <u>has swept</u> the floor.

2. You use the correct form of the verb 'to be,' making sure you use the correct tense, person and number:
    · The cleaner <u>is sweeping</u> the floor.
    · The cleaner <u>will be sweeping</u> the floor.

Fragments that are not complete thoughts and do not make sense by themselves:

A sentence or clause must make sense in the absence of any other writing.
    1. Even though she studied very diligently.
    2. Even though she studied very diligently, <u>she did not pass the exam</u>.

In the first sentence we do not know the result that answers 'even though', and therefore it is a fragment.

Exercise 7d

Rewrite the following sentences to correct the fragment. Check your answers with the answer key at the back of the book.

1 Cats like to play with balls, whereas dogs.

....

....

2 David playing tennis at the moment.

....

....

3 The sun has been all day.

....

....

4 Steven is very absent-minded. Always forgets to bring his workbooks.

....

....

5 We watching the movie yesterday when the accident at the cinema occurred.

....

....

4. Run-ons

A run-on sentence is a sentence that tries to join two 'complete sentences' together incorrectly. Remember, a 'complete sentence' (or an independent clause) has a subject, a verb and forms a complete idea. To join two 'complete sentences' together you can use a coordinating conjunction with a comma, a subordinating conjunction with a comma, a semicolon, or a period.

Let's look at a run-on sentence:

☹ Chloe takes the train to work Brian takes the bus.

This has two 'complete sentences' ("Chloe takes the train to work" and "Brian takes the bus"), but a coordinating conjunction, a subordinating conjunction, or a semicolon has not been used.

▶ A coordinating conjunction is used to join together two complete sentences that have equal standing in the sentence.
The coordinating conjunctions are:

> Coordinating conjunctions:
> **for** – to show cause
> **and** – to show addition
> **but, yet** – to show contrast
> **so** – to show effect
> **nor, or** – to show choice

So, if you want to correct the sentence and give equal importance to both 'complete' sentences you can insert a comma and use the appropriate coordinating conjunction:

☺ Chloe takes the train to work, but Brian takes the bus.

In this sentence there is equal emphasis on Chloe and Brian.

▶ A subordinating conjunction is used to join together two complete sentences in which one of the sentences is more important than the other sentence. The subordinating conjunctions are:

<u>Subordinating conjunctions:</u>
because, since - to show cause
although, while, even though, even if, whereas, though - to show contrast
so that, in that, in order that - to show effect
if, unless, provided that – to show condition

So, if you want to correct the sentence and give more importance to one of the 'complete' sentences you can insert a comma and use the appropriate subordinating conjunction:

☺ Chloe takes the train to work<u>, whereas</u> Brian takes the bus.

In this sentence there is more emphasis on Chloe.

▶ The third way to correct a run-on sentence is to use a semicolon, but you can only use this if the two 'complete sentences' share a common idea or a strong relationship.

☺ Chloe takes the train to work; Brian takes the bus.

However, the following sentence is incorrect because there is no direct relationship between the points:

☹ Chloe takes the train to work; Brian likes soccer.

▶ The final way to fix a run-on sentence is to use a period to separate the two sentences:

☺ Chloe takes the train to work. Brian takes the bus.

Rewrite the following sentences to correct the run-on.
Check your answers with the answer key at the back of the book.

1 The phone has broken we need to get a new one.

....

2 I do not have access to the Internet I am going to a PC room.

....

3 Flowers are lovely mosquitoes are horrible.

....

4 The TV show host is very funny he always signs autographs.

....

5 I love eating ice cream my brother is studying at university.

....

5. Comma splices

A comma splice is a type of run-on sentence that tries to join two 'complete sentences' together just with a comma. By itself, a comma is not adequate to join two 'complete sentences.'

The following sentence is a comma splice:

☹ I went to bed early last night, I did not watch the game.

To fix a comma splice you can use exactly the same techniques that are used to fix run-on sentences:

▶ You can keep the two clauses joined by using a coordinating conjunction with a comma, a subordinating conjunction with a comma, or a semicolon.

☺ I went to bed early last night, so I did not watch the game.

☺ I went to bed early last night, so that I did not watch the game.

☺ I went to bed early last night; I did not watch the game.

▶ Or you can separate the two clauses

☺ I went to bed early last night. I did not watch the game.

Rewrite the following sentences to correct the comma splice.
Check your answers with the answer key at the back of the book.

1 He can't afford to buy the car, it is too expensive.

....

2 I love eating, it is not one of my favorite hobbies.

....

3 Tom went into the supermarket, Lee went into the hotel.

....

4 The teacher is too strict, sometimes she is kind.

....

5 The museum is very interesting, it has the largest pottery collection in Asia.

....

Writing Focus

Unity

You have already looked at making sure that each paragraph only contains one main idea or theme, and that is one of the key elements to making sure there is <u>unity</u> in your writing.

Unity means that each paragraph should only contain one idea or point, and that everything you write in that paragraph is directly related to the topic sentence.

A key skill in writing with unity is being able to spot and eliminate anything that is not relevant. Look at this example:

> The ability to read is more important than the ability to write. Reading and writing are skills that are needed in everyday life; it is almost impossible to go through just one day without needing to read or write.

This passage lacks unity. The topic sentence states that <u>reading is more important than writing</u>, but the second sentence does not support this viewpoint; it talks about reading and writing on equal terms. Therefore the second sentence is not completely relevant to the topic and should be discarded.

Look at these passages written by Korean students of English. Highlight the parts that do not display unity:

1

Firstly, we can know that pyramids were built as a tomb of king. They represent just one point in the evolution of tomb design and records of them clearly indicated say so. But many people want to understand about the unreality about pyramids that could have required almost 360,000 workers over 20 years to build.

2

Nowadays, most people use a mobile phone. In various field, people get advantage of mobile phone. For examples, mobile phone is used to connecting near person, helping person who face on the emergency, working the business and promising an event, etc. For example, young people don't know about using the mobile phone in the right methods, but many young people or children use the mobile phone early too. It is social problem. Without a mobile phone life could be much harder, especially business working and emergency.

Coherence

If all parts of a piece of writing are connected, everything is understandable, and it all works toward a single conclusion or objective, the writing is <u>coherent</u>. Each sentence should 'flow' into the next sentence in terms of content, style and tone. Likewise, each paragraph should flow logically into the next.

Three key skills for achieving coherence are:

❶ Transitions   ❷ Logical organization   ❸ Repetition of key nouns

❶ Transitions

You have already looked at the use of transitions in Unit 4. To achieve coherence use transitions to move smoothly from one idea to the next, from one sentence to the next, and from one paragraph to the next.

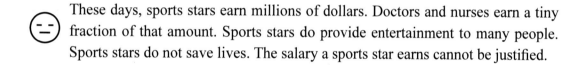 These days, sports stars earn millions of dollars. Doctors and nurses earn a tiny fraction of that amount. Sports stars do provide entertainment to many people. Sports stars do not save lives. The salary a sports star earns cannot be justified.

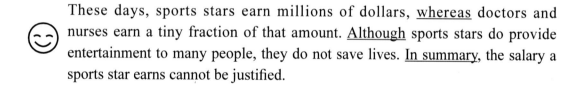 These days, sports stars earn millions of dollars, <u>whereas</u> doctors and nurses earn a tiny fraction of that amount. <u>Although</u> sports stars do provide entertainment to many people, they do not save lives. <u>In summary</u>, the salary a sports star earns cannot be justified.

❷ Logical organization

How you organize your writing is an important factor in achieving coherence, and the main emphasis must be on making your writing logical. Look at this example:

A piece of land can be used in many ways, and one of the best ways to utilize land is to build something worthwhile and useful.
The land can also be used for agriculture or can be turned into a conservation area. Schools, hospitals, libraries and parks are positive and helpful constructions that can be built on land.

This passage is not logical or organized. The first sentence is about using the land to build something. The second sentence is about other possible uses of the land, and the third sentence is back to examples of what could be built. A more logical organization would be:

A piece of land can be used in many ways, and one of the best ways to utilize land is to build something worthwhile and useful. Schools, hospitals, libraries and parks are positive and helpful constructions that can be built on land. Alternatively, the land can also be used for agriculture or can be turned into a conservation area.

Some common ways to organize your writing are:

• Order of importance. Put the most important point first, then the next most important, etc.
• Chronological order. Put your points in the order they happened or occurred.
• General to specific. Put your high level points first, and then get more and more specific with your detail.
• By proportion of relevance. Use more words for the items of most importance and less words for secondary items.

❸ Repetition of key nouns

A common error in essays is repetition of statements and ideas. As long as you have clearly stated your point, explained it fully and validated it, there is no need to repeat the same point again.

However, one type of repetition can aid cohesion in your writing. By repeating key nouns you create a common thread that allows the reader to completely understand exactly what you are trying to say.

Of course, if you repeat the same noun too many times, the writing becomes dull and poorly written, therefore you must use pronouns and synonyms appropriately. A rule to follow is that whenever using a pronoun or a synonym might cause confusion, you should instead repeat the key noun.

For instance:

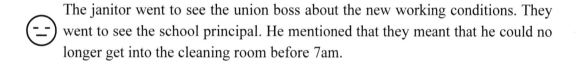 The janitor went to see the union boss about the new working conditions. They went to see the school principal. He mentioned that they meant that he could no longer get into the cleaning room before 7am.

This passage is confusing because pronouns have replaced too many key nouns. By repeating key nouns the passage becomes much clearer:

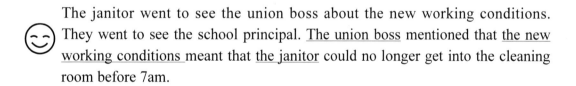 The janitor went to see the union boss about the new working conditions. They went to see the school principal. The union boss mentioned that the new working conditions meant that the janitor could no longer get into the cleaning room before 7am.

A Korean student of English wrote the following passage. The use of English is good but it lacks cohesion. Rewrite this passage using the three key skills of cohesion (transitions, logical organization and repetition of key nouns). A sample answer is provided at the back of the book.

Actually doing something is the key to acquiring knowledge. Family and friends can be good advisors. The advice is often ignored. When a person listens to the lesson from them, they cannot truly be aware of it 'under the skin.' Once they confront the actual situation, they will perceive it by themselves and it becomes fixed. There is no substitute for learning by experience.

....

....

....

....

....

....

....

....

Unit 9 Academic Writing

In Unit 6 you looked at some aspects of writing academically:

  • avoiding clichés
  • avoiding euphemisms
  • avoiding informal language such as colloquialisms

In addition, there are some more guidelines you need to follow in academic writing.

1. Write in the third person, or write impersonally

You should avoid writing in the first and second person:

☹ First person: *I (/we)* saved the water supply by cleaning the blockage.
☹ Second person: *You* saved the water supply by cleaning the blockage.

The third person voice can be used, but avoid using informal pronouns such as he, she, it and they too often. You can sometimes use the noun rather than the pronoun to make your writing more 'academic':

☺ Third person: *The team* saved the water supply by cleaning the blockage.

Writing impersonally states the facts and does not necessarily include detail about the person or entity involved:

☺ Impersonal: *Cleaning the blockage* saved the water supply.

Rewrite the following sentences in either the third person or impersonally. See the answer key at the back of the book for sample answers.

1 He should not accept a place at university unless he is prepared to work hard.

....

....

....

2 We did not discover sufficient evidence linking acid rain to skin problems.

....

....

....

3 If you smoke you increase your risk of developing heart disease and lung cancer.

....

....

....

4 My parents are the best teachers for me because they know exactly how I learn and the pace at which I can study.

....

....

....

5 I would use a sample of Hangul, the Korean alphabet, as something symbolic and representative of my country.

....

....

....

2. Do not use contractions

Contractions are a combined and shortened form of two different words. Contractions are common in speech, but are too informal for academic writing. Instead of writing the contraction you must write the two words individually.

For example:

'won't' should be written as 'will not'
'couldn't' should be written as 'could not'
'it's' should be written as 'it is'

Exercise 9b

Write the individual two words that form each contraction.

1 what've

....

2 doesn't

....

3 weren't

....

4 let's

....

5 what's

....

A list of common contractions is provided at the end of this unit.

The next two guidelines are relevant if you are writing essays for college or university assignments. If you are studying English to take an exam such as TOEFL or IELTS you must make sure you do not plagiarize, but you will not need to cite or create a reference list/bibliography.

3. Do not plagiarize and cite correctly

Plagiarism is the act of pretending that the words or ideas that you have used in your essay are your own, when in fact you have copied them from someone else. Plagiarism can be deliberate (when you intentionally pretend you wrote something but you have copied it from somewhere), or accidental (when you did not mean to pretend the words or ideas are yours).

The main way to avoid plagiarism is to cite the source text. You need to cite the source if:
- you use the ideas or content from someone else's work, even if you paraphrase the passage.
- you use a direct quotation from a source text.
- you copy more than two or three consecutive words from a source text.

Citing means to acknowledge the original passage in your essay. There are many different styles of citing, and a search on the Internet using 'citing' will bring up a list. One of the most common styles of citation is called the Harvard System, and this is the type of citing we will look at in this book.

The Harvard System of citing uses 'in-text' citation in the format of (author, date). The three most important rules in using the Harvard style are:

1) Using ideas or information from a source text
If you are mentioning the source text but are not directly quoting or paraphrasing you just use the author's family name and the year of the publication of the book. For instance:

Malnutrition was shown to be the major factor (Bosdet, 1998). In contrast (Miller, 2003) suggests that poor sanitation was the most significant reason.

More than one person often writes books and research, so you need to cite in the following way:

2 authors: (Hurst & Moore, 1966)
More than 2 authors: (Charlton et al., 1966)

Note: et al is Latin – it means 'and others.'

2) Paraphrasing passages from a source text

If you paraphrase a passage, you can introduce the paraphrase using a slightly different way of citing. Some common ways to begin a cited paraphrase are:

According to Roberts (1975)...
Research by Roberts (1975) suggested that...
Roberts (1975) stated that...

3) Using quotations from a source text

There are two ways to cite direct quotations, and they both require you to add the page number (author, date, page number):

• If the quotation you are using is short you must use quotation marks:

As stated, "changing the role of politicians could lead to anarchy" (Mildew 1999, p.58)

• If the quotation is long you must indent the quotation, but do not use quotation marks:

People attend university for many reasons

Students go to university to gain knowledge, to acquire social skills, to increase their career prospects and importantly, to have some fun. (Morris 2004, p.123)

and it is often for very personal reasons.

Copy this passage in the space below, adding the correct citations using the information below the passage. Check your answer with the answer key at the back of the book.

According to David Bartholomew the reason developing countries cannot escape poverty is because rich countries will not agree to reduce the debt burden. It has been said, "Rich countries need to write off some of the debt that poorer countries owe; otherwise the poorer country can never escape the cycle of having to borrow more money to grow its economy." Likewise, the amount of interest paid by developing countries to developed countries has tripled in the last ten years.

Information:

Paraphrase taken from: Bartholomew, D., (2003), Why Debt Matters, New York, XYZ Books

Quotation "Rich countries need ... its economy" taken from page 216 from 'An unfair world' written by Roberts, Jones and Smith in 2002.

Information about interest paid by developing countries extracted from an article written by Amanda Burgess for the Weekly Review in April 2001.

4. Create a reference list and a bibliography

The reference list is a list of all the citations in your essay, and you create a reference list at the end of your essay.
The reference list should be in alphabetical order of the author's family name.

The details you need to provide in a reference list differ depending on the type of text you have cited:

A book:	author, date, *title*, where published, publisher
e.g.	Wills, K *et al.*, (1888), *The Best Book*, London, Best Publishing Ltd
Chapter in a book:	author, date, chapter title, *book title*, page range, where published, publisher
e.g.	Wills, K et al., (1888), The Best Chapter, *The Best Book*, pp 50-85, London, Best Publishing Ltd
A journal:	author, date, article title, *journal title*, volume number, page range
e.g.	London, G., (2005), UFO sightings, *UFO Times*, 29, pp 23-25
The Internet:	author, date (if known), article title, website address, date you visited the website
e.g.	Passmore, A. (2011). TESOL explained, www.tesol.org/xyz/pass.html, Feb 12th, 2011

A bibliography is a list of all the resources you have read as background reading, but have not cited, in your essay.

The format of listing a bibliography is the same as for a reference list; you produce the bibliography in alphabetical order of the author's family name and use the format and information as shown for the reference list (i.e. author, date, title, etc.).

If you have read more than one book by the same author, put them in alphabetical order of the title:

Elliot, M., (2000), Great Works, Seoul, SB Publishing
Elliot, M., (1993), Highest Works, Seoul, SB Publishing

Remember, the bibliography should only contain the texts you have read, but have not cited, in your essay. The reference list must contain all the texts you have cited.

Exercise 9d

Create a correctly ordered and formatted bibliography using the following details. Check your answer with the answer key at the back of the book.

A book called The Way to Go, published in Paris by FRP Company. Written by David Pierre in 2001

A book written by David Pierre in 2010 called On My Own. Published by QWE Books Ltd of Vancouver

An Internet article from tagose.com, which was written and looked at in Feb 2011. Called 'Why I am here' by J.R. Bolden

....

....

....

....

....

....

Further Practice

A Korean student of English wrote this essay. Read through the student's essay and highlight parts that are not written academically. There is a note section at the end for you to write your ideas and comments.

These days, most of people eager to be employed by big companies, and they just don't consider about the jobs in smaller ones. It's considered as a failure to get a job in small company. I don't think so. I agree that big companies' employees are much more stable and high-payed. But small companies also have their own advantages. They're more creative and easier to get promotion.

First, small companies are creative. Normally, big companies have their own rules, the rules that must be followed. In this condition, it's hard to think any inventive ideas, because every works should be matched with the rule. On the other hands, small companies yet don't have these rules, so it's natural that they're much more creative and flexible. It helps employees to work more efficiently. In this consequence, they can work with no pressure, and it leads to many constructive ideas that work for company. For example, Google, one of the biggest searching engine company provided fabulous environment to its employees, for its own sake.

Also, we can promote much faster than big companies, if we are in small ones. In fact, it involves one of disadvantages that small companies have. Fast promotion means unstability of the jobs. But, if we use the chances properly and prove our ability, we are able to promote higher than we expected.

In conclusion, I prefer small companies because it's more creative and easy to promote.

Your notes:

Contractions that should be avoided in academic writing:

Contraction	Should be written as:	Contraction	Should be written as:
aren't	are not	that's	that is; that has
can't	cannot	there's	there is; there has
couldn't	could not	they'd	they had; they would
didn't	did not	they'll	they will; they shall
doesn't	does not	they're	they are
don't	do not	they've	they have
hadn't	had not	we'd	we had; we would
hasn't	has not	we're	we are
haven't	have not	we've	we have
he'd	he had; he would	weren't	were not
he'll	he will; he shall	what'll	what will; what shall
he's	he is; he has	what're	what are
I'd	I had; I would	what's	what is; what has
I'll	I will; I shall	what've	what have
I'm	I am	where's	where is; where has
I've	I have	who'd	who had; who would
isn't	is not	who'll	who will; who shall
let's	let us	who's	who is; who has
mightn't	might not	who've	who have
mustn't	must not	won't	will not
shan't	shall not	wouldn't	would not
she'd	she had; she would	you'd	you had; you would
she'll	she will; she shall	you'll	you will; you shall
she's	she is; she has	you're	you are
shouldn't	should not	you've	you have

Answers
with Explanations STEP1

Exercise 1a ▶ see p. 17

❶ The question asks whether you agree or disagree that language and culture are less respected now than in the past. The answer focuses on the fact that language and culture should be respected, but does not include the comparison between now and the past.

❷ a
⇨The question asks you to choose to agree or choose to disagree, not to do both.

Exercise 1b ▶ see p. 20

❶ opinion
⇨The question asks you to give your opinion on whether this change has improved people's lives.

❷ cause/effect
⇨This question also asks for solutions by asking you to explain what could be done to reduce traffic accidents.

❸ advantages/disadvantages & preference
⇨You would need to explain both the benefits and drawbacks of the new factory, and then give your preference as to whether you want the factory to be built or not.

❹ agree/disagree
⇨Nearly every agree/disagree question will actually contain the words 'agree' and 'disagree.'

❺ preference
⇨The question is asking for your choice, and if you choose something you prefer it to the alternative.

❻ compare/contrast
⇨Most questions in this type of essay will use the words 'compare' and 'contrast.'

Exercise 1c ▶ see p. 23

❶ Answers will vary. Some suggestions are provided below:

> **Agree or disagree: Disagree**
> **Ideas:**
> Language constantly evolves > does not mean disrespect
> Many countries fight to keep own language despite spread of English these days.
>
> Governments nowadays spend lots of money to preserve cultural assets
> and places of interest.
> People in hectic modern society appreciate tradition > more museums, etc. nowadays

❷ Answers will vary.

Exercise 1d ▶ see p. 25

Introduction	Thesis statement:	Online shopping has many advantages–goods are getting cheaper and cheaper; benefits the environment.
Body paragraph 1	Topic sentence:	Less overheads therefore goods are cheaper.
	Detail:	Because goods are cheaper people can have lower-paid jobs and still be able to buy things.
Body paragraph 2	Transition:	Secondly,
	Topic sentence:	Online shopping is good for the environment.
	Detail:	Less packaging and less shoppers traveling.
Conclusion	Summarize your opinion or suggest a solution	Online shopping is definitely increasing and is good.

⇨ The question is not asking about the advantages of online shopping. To directly answer the question there should be a paragraph about how the increase affects the environment, and a paragraph about how the increase affects the type of jobs required. The conclusion needs to mention the two items (effect on environment and effect on type of job), and not give an opinion whether online shopping is definitely increasing.

Exercise 1e ▶ see p. 26

Answers will vary.

Introduction	**Thesis statement:**	Language and culture are still respected. Language evolves naturally to reflect modern times, but this is not disrespect. Governments would not spend lots of money these days to protect cultural assets if culture was valued less than in the past.
Body paragraph 1	**Topic sentence:**	As times change and new technology is introduced it is natural that language alters.
	Detail:	Text messaging, email, and the Internet have their own language, but Shakespeare is not changed; it is still respected.
Body paragraph 2	**Transition:**	Likewise,
	Topic sentence:	If respect for culture was diminished then public money would not be spent on preserving temples and monuments.
	Detail:	Food, traditional industries, buildings are all protected.
Conclusion	**Summarize your opinion or suggest a solution**	In sum, it is not true that language and culture are respected less now than in the past.

Exercise 1f ▶ see p. 28

Item	YES	NO
Does the thesis statement directly answer the question?		✓
Does everything in the essay support the thesis statement?		✓
Have all the components of an essay been included, such as topic sentences, a conclusion, etc.?	✓	
Has the writer avoided repeating a point more than once?		✓
Do all the points follow a logical order?	✓	

⇨ The thesis statement is a little unclear. Although it does convey the idea that smoking should be banned it could be much more direct. The points in both body paragraphs are valid, but they have not been explicitly mentioned in the thesis statement. The logic of the second body paragraph is flawed; the topic sentence is about the effect on children seeing smokers but the support mentions exposure to nicotine (which was already mentioned in the first body paragraph).

Exercise 1g ▶ see p. 29

Online shopping could contribute to protecting the environment from pollution. In fact, all environmental components, such as fresh water, air and soil are polluted by the large number of vehicles on the roads. Online shopping would discourage people from using their vehicles, because the Internet allows shoppers to search for and purchase what they want at home. For example, if people do not go to shopping outside, the amount of time spent using cars, buses, and taxis would be decreased. People could help nature by shopping online.

Unit 2 | Writing the Introduction

Exercise 2a ▶ see p. 34

1

Opening sentence	YES	NO
Is there some background or general information about the main topic of the question?		√
Is there a 'hook' to get the reader's attention?		√
Thesis statement	**YES**	**NO**
Does it directly answer the question and clearly state the topic of the essay?	√	
Does it clearly state the writer's opinion and make a claim that others might disagree with?	√	
Does it tell the reader what to expect in the rest of the essay?	√	

2

Opening sentence	YES	NO
Is there some background or general information about the main topic of the question?		√
Is there a 'hook' to get the reader's attention?	√	
Thesis statement	**YES**	**NO**
Does it directly answer the question and clearly state the topic of the essay?	√	
Does it clearly state the writer's opinion and make a claim that others might disagree with?	√	
Does it tell the reader what to expect in the rest of the essay?	√	

Exercise 2b ▶ see p. 39

❶ a

⇨ Sentence b) has changed a few words slightly, but the basic word pattern and structure are the same as the source text.

❷ b

⇨ Sentence a) has slightly altered the meaning of the source text. 'understand' and 'consider' from the two sentences have different meanings, and the synonyms chosen for 'logical thinking' and 'determination' are not quite correct.

❸ b

⇨ Sentence a) has added information that is not in the source text. From the source text we do not know that Asian people did not like beer.

Exercise 2c ▶ see p. 40

Answers will vary.

❶ The Art department and the English department should receive equal funding from the university.

❷ Growing up in a big city is less beneficial to children than growing up in the countryside.

❸ Companies frequently test products using cruel and unwarranted experiments on animals.

Exercise 2d ▶ see p. 41

❶ b

⇨Sentence a) is vague, it fails to give an opinion, and the reader does not know what to expect from the rest of the essay.

❷ b

⇨Sentence a) uses the word 'could,' which does not give the reader the author's opinion. Also, sentence a) gives two potential topics: the essay could be about a business utilizing the Internet, or it could be about two reasons why a well-desinged web page is a good advertisement.

❸ b

⇨ Sentence a) is vague, it does not give specific details that others might dispute.

Exercise 2e ▶ see p. 42

Answers will vary.

❶ **The world of fashion changed dramatically in the 1920s. Women discarded restrictive corsets and enjoyed more freedom in their attire, and men abandoned formal wear in favour of sports clothes. We can see the influence of 1920s fashion in the more casual style of clothing worn today.**

❷ **While downsizing can give some short-term benefits to a company, in the long-term downsizing is not an effective business strategy as it de-motivates staff and decreases production capacity.**

❸ **The fact that food is now much easier to prepare than it was in the past has definitely improved people's lives. Firstly, people have more free-time and secondly, they can try to cook more exotic and delicious dishes.**

Exercise 3a ▶ see p. 47

Topic sentence	YES	NO
Is the topic sentence a summary of what the paragraph will be about?		√
Does it control the paragraph?		√
Has it excluded details?		√

⇨ The text does not concisely tell the reader the one main idea of the paragraph and it contains too much detail.

Topic sentence	YES	NO
Is the topic sentence a summary of what the paragraph will be about?	√	
Does it control the paragraph?	√	
Has it excluded details?	√	

Exercise 3b ▶ see p. 50

Concluding sentence	YES	NO
Is the concluding sentence directly related to the topic sentence?	√	
Does it rephrase the topic sentence without adding new information?	√	
Does it avoid simply re-writing what has already been stated?	√	

Concluding sentence	YES	NO
Is the concluding sentence directly related to the topic sentence?		√
Does it rephrase the topic sentence without adding new information?		√
Does it avoid simply re-writing what has already been stated?	√	

⇨ Collocations might be an example within the body paragraph, but it is not directly related to the topic sentence about feedback.

Exercise 3c ▶ see p. 55

❶ a

⇨ Sentence b) has two points–free tuition and no distinction between international and domestic students.

❷ b

⇨ Sentence a) has two points–being trustworthy is different from hardworking. A paragraph should have one main idea.

❸ a

⇨ Sentence b) is further detail, not a topic sentence.

Exercise 3d ▶ see p. 56

Answers will vary.

❶ For men in the 1920s, casual sports wear became more popular than formal attire.

❷ The main reason that downsizing is not a viable long-term strategy is that it demotivates employees.

❸ In addition, people are now able to try more adventurous styles of cooking because food is easier to prepare.

Exercise 3e ▶ see p. 58

❶ Often, if people do not combine a diet with an exercise program or a change of eating habits, they simply regain weight immediately upon the cessation of their diet.

❷ The evidence suggests that the sea level is rising as a direct result of global warming. Two pieces of research have concluded that in the last 10 years the sea level has dramatically increased, and that ozone layer deterioration is melting the Antarctic sea glaciers at an alarming rate.

❸ It is clear that companies have too much leeway in how they advertise their products. They can easily make disingenuous claims that can particularly affect the vulnerable members of society. Regulation must be tightened.

Exercise 4a ▶ see p. 68

Paragraph	YES	NO
Does the paragraph contain only one position or argument?		√
Is there a strong topic sentence?	√	
Is the topic sentence 'expanded and explained' in the next few sentences?		√
Is the position or opinion 'reinforced'?	√	
Is there sufficient 'validation' of the position or argument?	√	
Is there a strong concluding sentence?		√

⇨ There are two points in this paragraph–equal treatment and chances to learn. The topic about being treated equally is reasonably strong, but the expansion becomes confused due to the inclusion of the point about 'chances to learn.' Even though the point about being treated equally is not really reinforced, it is validated by an example.

②

Paragraph	YES	NO
Does the paragraph contain only one position or argument?	√	
Is there a strong topic sentence?	√	
Is the topic sentence 'expanded and explained' in the next few sentences?	√	
Is the position or opinion 'reinforced'?	√	
Is there sufficient 'validation' of the position or argument?	√	
Is there a strong concluding sentence?	√	

Exercise 4b ▶ see p. 75

These answers provide one possibility. For some questions there may be more than one viable answer.

1 **The swimming pool became dirty <u>because</u> nobody cleaned it.**

2 **<u>Even though</u> exercise is good for me, I prefer watching TV.**

3 **Acid rain is harmful to the environment. <u>Likewise</u>, deforestation is also bad for the planet.**

4 **Too much cultural diversity in a city can cause challenges. <u>For example</u>, there are some schools in London that have to provide learning material in five or more languages.**

5 **Environmental conditions in some countries are stable, <u>whereas</u> other countries suffer from all kinds of environmental problems.**

6 **Video games are detrimental to a child's development. Firstly, they take too much of a child's time, and <u>furthermore</u> they have very little educational merit.**

Exercise 4c ▶ see p. 77

1 **b**
⇨Sentence a) is just a restatement of the topic sentence.

2 **b**
⇨Sentence a) is not directly related to improving young people's health.

3 **b**
⇨Sentence a) is not directly related to equal roles and it is not verifiable.

Exercise 4d ▶ see p. 78

Answers will vary.

1 Statistics from the Someland Bureau of Facts released in 2010 illustrate this point. The statistics showed that 33% of marriages ended in divorce in 2008, compared to only 10% in 1996.

2 This point can be summed up in the old Spanish proverb, "A wise man changes his mind, but a fool never will."

3 For example, my father has a mundane job working in a factory so at weekends he goes scuba diving. He says that the excitement of going diving at the weekends keeps him motivated at work.

Unit 5 | Writing the Conclusion

Exercise 5a ▶ see p. 88

1

	YES	NO
Is there a clear 'conclusion transition'?	√	
Does the first sentence directly answer the question?		√
Does the conclusion state the main arguments that support the writer's position on the topic?	√	
Does the conclusion contain a final comment?		√

2

	YES	NO
Is there a clear 'conclusion transition'?	√	
Does the first sentence directly answer the question?	√	
Does the conclusion state the main arguments that support the writer's position on the topic?	√	
Does the conclusion contain a final comment?		√

Exercise 5b ▶ see p. 92

1 This conclusion does not directly answer the question. The conclusion also contains minor details (sculpture, paintings, etc.). It also adds new information ('In addition to the points already mentioned').

2 This conclusion is too long and it probably restates too much of what is probably in the body paragraphs. Also, there is no final comment.

Exercise 5c ▶ see p. 95

First sentence of the conclusion to answer the question:	In conclusion, it is preferable to do work manually.
Paraphrase of the thesis statement:	By using their hands people get more satisfaction on completion of the task, and it is possible to make sure the work is completed properly.

First sentence of the conclusion to answer the question:	In summary, childhood obesity is rising due to poor diets and a lack of exercise.
Paraphrase of the thesis statement:	Weight gain and disease are direct consequences of eating junk food, and children do not maintain a healthy weight because they spend too much time inactive.

Exercise 6a   ▶ see p. 102

Answers will vary.

❶ After a hard day at work people deserve to take a rest.

❷ A bar of chocolate **contains too much sugar and fat.**

❸ Exams are too pressurized and examinees often run out of time.

❹ It is beneficial for young children to go abroad **to study.**

❺ Governments and environmental groups need to reach an agreement **quickly.**

Exercise 6b   ▶ see p. 103

❶ Children should not socialize **with people much older than them.**

❷ I became interested in **rock music while I was at university.**

❸ The comedian was great**, but his last joke** was not very good.

❹ Employees often make mistakes **at work.**

❺ Stress must not overwhelm **you.**

Exercise 6c   ▶ see p. 105

❶ Eating a poor diet can lead to obesity.

❷ Following fashion trends regularly stops people from studying and doing other important things.

❸ Watching too many movies stops a person from gaining essential social skills that are needed each and every day.

Exercise 6d ▶ see p. 107

❶ The age 20 to 25 will be the <mark>very</mark> busiest time in the life, <mark>it is much busier than other times of life such as 15-19.</mark> But among the things they should do, the most <mark>absolute</mark> important thing that they should do is to study lessons in the college. College is the first and maybe the last place that one can choose themselves the class that one want to study. The education in the college can decide one's field or career. <mark>Meaning, the college can decide one's future life.</mark>

❷ Second, the government spend a lot of money to educate students. Students have to go to school until middle school. While students go to middle school, government try to make good environment to study <mark>and make comfortable to study in the schools, it spends a lot of money.</mark>

Exercise 6e ▶ see p. 109

❶ Knowledge acquired from books is superior to knowledge gained from experience.

❷ At sports stadiums people are always crammed together.

❸ Too often, a teacher berates a student for something unimportant.

Exercise 6f ▶ see p. 111

Lucy's redundancy was a disgrace. Her removal from the board of directors was devastating to her, especially as her mother had recently died. She left the competitive world of business and went to live in the countryside. Many of her friends were jealous about her new lifestyle, but she soon became bored of it.

Exercise 6g ▶ see p. 113

❶ During the interview I realized that I would not get the job.

❷ The Principal decided to reduce the number of teachers.

❸ While writing an essay a student can learn many things.

Exercise 6h ▶ see p. 115

Answers may vary. A sample answer is provided below:

People should demonstrate more because a government needs to understand that people really do care. People need to protest so the government has incentive to change. Throughout history there are examples where public protest has led to change. For example, Martin Luther King. He led protests about civil rights and America is now a very different place.

Unit 7 Common Errors

Exercise 7a ▶ see p. 119

❶ **Each student must submit** his or her **homework by Friday.**
⇨Each student is singular.

❷ **The business released** its **results last week, but** the results **were very disappointing.**
⇨A business is singular, and the pronoun 'they' was not clearly referring to the results.

❸ **The tree fell onto the house, but amazingly** the house **was not damaged.**
⇨'it' could have been the house or the tree.

❹ **I don't like my feet.** They are **unattractive.**
⇨ Number agreement

❺ **If the children keep being naughty,** they **will be punished.**

Exercise 7b ▶ see p.120

Another experience awaits students in other countries; they **will live alone. From the exotic scenery and their lonely situation, they will appreciate the presence of** their **family and friends. Otherwise, they cannot easily recognize** the **importance** of their family **no matter how an acquaintance exhorts the young adults to treat their family well. Therefore, when** people **listen to the lesson from** their **family and friends, they cannot truly be aware of it.**

Exercise 7c ▶ see p. 122

In many countries <u>the</u> birth rate is falling. If this trend continues it will have <u>a</u> very big impact on society, because it will be harder for <u>a</u> government to look after <u>the</u> elderly. <u>An</u> older person needs <u>a</u> reasonable amount of income in order to live, but if there are less babies being born, eventually there will be <u>a</u> smaller workforce who can pay <u>the</u> taxes that can be used by <u>the</u> government to provide <u>a</u> pension to <u>the</u> older generation. <u>A</u> possible solution is to increase <u>the</u> rate of tax, but this will be <u>a</u> burden on <u>the</u> workforce which could even lead to social unrest.

Exercise 7d ▶ see p. 124

1 Cats like to play with balls, whereas dogs <u>like to play in water</u>.

2 David <u>is</u> playing tennis at the moment.

3 The sun has been <u>shining</u> all day.

4 Steven is very absent-minded. <u>He</u> always forgets to bring his workbooks.

5 We <u>were</u> watching the movie yesterday when the accident at the cinema occurred.

Exercise 7e ▶ see p. 128

There may be more than one correct answer.

1 The phone has broken <u>so</u> we need to get a new one.

2 I do not have access to the Internet<u>;</u> I am going to a PC room.

3 Flowers are lovely<u>, whereas</u> mosquitoes are horrible.

4 The TV show host is very funny <u>and</u> he always signs autographs.

5 I love eating ice cream<u>. My</u> brother is studying at university.

Exercise 7f ▶ see p. 130

1 He can't afford to buy the car; it is too expensive.

2 I love eating, <u>but</u> it is not one of my favorite hobbies.

3 Tom went into the supermarket, <u>while</u> Lee went into the hotel.

4 The teacher is too strict, <u>although</u> sometimes she is kind.

5 The museum is very interesting. <u>It</u> has the largest pottery collection in Asia.

Unit 8   Unity and Coherence

Exercise 8a ▶ see p. 132

1 Firstly, we can know that pyramids were built as a tomb of king. They represent just one point in the evolution of tomb design and records of them clearly indicated say so. But many people want to understand about the unreality about pyramids that could have required almost 360,000 workers over 20 years to build.

⇨ The topic sentence is about the function of a pyramid (a king's tomb). The highlighted sentence is about how pyramids were constructed.

2 Nowadays, most people use a mobile phone. In various field, people get advantage of mobile phone. For examples, mobile phone is used to connecting near person, helping person who face on the emergency, working the business and promising an event, etc. For example, young people don't know about using the mobile phone in the right methods, but many young people or children use the mobile phone early too. It is social problem. Without a mobile phone life could be much harder, especially business working and emergency.

⇨ The main theme of this passage is the advantages of a mobile phone. But the example about young people not knowing how to use a mobile phone properly is not relevant to the topic.

Exercise 8b ▶ see p. 136

Actually doing something is the key to acquiring knowledge <u>and</u> <mark>there is no substitute for learning by experience</mark>. Family and friends can be good advisors <u>but</u> the advice is often ignored. When a person listens to the lesson from <u>their family and friends,</u> the <u>person</u> cannot truly be aware of the <u>lesson</u> 'under the skin.' <u>However</u>, once <u>a person</u> confronts the actual situation, <u>he or she</u> will perceive the <u>lesson</u> himself or herself and <u>it</u> becomes fixed.

⇨ <u>Colored words underlined</u> = transitions added
⇨ <mark>Highlighting</mark> = organizational change
⇨ <u>Underlined</u> = key noun repetition and appropriate pronoun use

Unit 9   Academic Writing

Exercise 9a   ▶ see p. 138

❶ A place at university should not be accepted unless the person is prepared to work hard.

❷ Insufficient evidence was found linking acid rain to skin problems.

❸ Smoking increases the risk of developing heart disease and lung cancer.

❹ Parents are the best teachers for their children as parents know how their children learn and the pace at which their children study.

❺ Hangul, the Korean alphabet, would be a good symbol representing Korea.

Exercise 9b   ▶ see p. 140

❶ what have   ❷ does not   ❸ were not

❹ let us   ❺ what is

Exercise 9c ▶ see p. 144

According to Bartholomew (2003) the reason developing countries cannot escape poverty is because rich countries will not agree to reduce the debt burden. It has been said,

> Rich countries need to write off some of the debt that poorer countries owe; otherwise the poorer country can never escape the cycle of having to borrow more money to grow its economy.
> (Roberts et al 2002, p. 216)

Likewise, the amount of interest paid by developing countries to developed countries has tripled in the last ten years (Burgess, 2001).

Exercise 9d ▶ see p. 147

Bolden, J.R., Why I am here, www.tagose.com, Feb 2011

Pierre, D., (2010), On My Own, Vancouver, QWE Books Ltd

Pierre, D., (2001), The Way to Go, Paris, FRP Company